Matlab Programming: A Comprehensive Guide For Beginners

Anshuman Mishra

Published by Anshuman Mishra, 2025.

ABOUT THE BOOK:

"MATLAB PROGRAMMING: A COMPREHENSIVE GUIDE FOR BEGINNERS" IS A WELL-STRUCTURED AND PRACTICAL GUIDE DESIGNED TO HELP LEARNERS MASTER MATLAB PROGRAMMING WHILE SIMULTANEOUSLY GAINING INSIGHTS INTO C PROGRAMMING. THIS BOOK OFFERS A SMOOTH TRANSITION FOR THOSE FAMILIAR WITH C WHO WISH TO UNDERSTAND MATLAB, MAKING IT IDEAL FOR STUDENTS, ENGINEERS, RESEARCHERS, AND ANYONE INTERESTED IN NUMERICAL COMPUTING, DATA ANALYSIS, AND SIMULATION USING MATLAB.

THE BOOK STARTS WITH THE BASICS OF PROGRAMMING, MOVING THROUGH CORE MATLAB CONCEPTS SUCH AS VARIABLES, FUNCTIONS, ARRAYS, PLOTTING, AND CONTROL FLOW, AND CULMINATES IN MORE ADVANCED TOPICS LIKE DATA MANIPULATION, OPTIMIZATION, AND REAL-WORLD CASE STUDIES. ALONG THE WAY, READERS WILL ENCOUNTER PROGRAMMING EXAMPLES THAT ARE ROOTED IN BOTH MATLAB AND C, ALLOWING THEM TO SEE HOW SIMILAR TASKS ARE PERFORMED IN BOTH LANGUAGES, AND LEARN HOW TO MAKE THE BEST USE OF MATLAB'S POWERFUL BUILT-IN FUNCTIONS.

EACH CHAPTER INCLUDES CLEAR EXPLANATIONS, HANDS-ON PROGRAMMING EXERCISES, AND CASE STUDIES DESIGNED TO DEMONSTRATE REAL-WORLD APPLICATIONS. THE BOOK AIMS TO BUILD A SOLID FOUNDATION IN MATLAB, WHILE LEVERAGING THE READER'S KNOWLEDGE OF C PROGRAMMING TO ENHANCE THEIR LEARNING EXPERIENCE AND BROADEN THEIR PROGRAMMING SKILL SET.

BENEFITS OF STUDYING THIS BOOK:

1. **BRIDGING MATLAB AND C PROGRAMMING**
   THIS BOOK PROVIDES A UNIQUE OPPORTUNITY FOR READERS WITH A BACKGROUND IN C PROGRAMMING TO UNDERSTAND MATLAB AND SEE HOW THE TWO LANGUAGES COMPARE. BY TRANSLATING C CODE INTO MATLAB, LEARNERS CAN REINFORCE THEIR KNOWLEDGE OF PROGRAMMING WHILE LEARNING NEW, POWERFUL MATLAB TECHNIQUES.

2. **CLEAR STRUCTURE FOR BEGINNERS**
   THE CHAPTERS ARE THOUGHTFULLY ORGANIZED TO BEGIN WITH FOUNDATIONAL CONCEPTS AND PROGRESS TO MORE COMPLEX TOPICS. EACH CHAPTER BUILDS ON THE PREVIOUS ONE, HELPING YOU GRADUALLY DEEPEN YOUR UNDERSTANDING WITHOUT FEELING OVERWHELMED.

3. **HANDS-ON PRACTICE AND EXERCISES**
   THE BOOK INCLUDES NUMEROUS PRACTICE PROBLEMS, CASE STUDIES, AND REAL-WORLD EXAMPLES THAT WILL REINFORCE THE CONCEPTS INTRODUCED IN EACH CHAPTER. THE EXERCISES ARE DESIGNED TO HELP YOU APPLY WHAT YOU'VE LEARNED AND DEVELOP YOUR SKILLS IN A PRACTICAL MANNER.

4. **COMPREHENSIVE COVERAGE**
   FROM BASIC PROGRAMMING CONCEPTS LIKE VARIABLES, ARRAYS, AND CONTROL FLOW TO ADVANCED TOPICS LIKE DATA VISUALIZATION, OPTIMIZATION, AND FILE HANDLING, THIS BOOK COVERS THE KEY AREAS OF MATLAB PROGRAMMING. IT ALSO INTRODUCES IMPORTANT CONCEPTS IN C PROGRAMMING, ALLOWING YOU TO SEE THE RELATIONSHIP BETWEEN THE TWO LANGUAGES.

5. **MATLAB AS A TOOL FOR ENGINEERS AND SCIENTISTS**
   MATLAB IS WIDELY USED IN ENGINEERING, DATA SCIENCE, AND RESEARCH. THIS BOOK WILL TEACH YOU HOW TO USE MATLAB FOR NUMERICAL COMPUTATION, SIMULATIONS, AND DATA ANALYSIS, SKILLS THAT ARE ESSENTIAL FOR TACKLING REAL-WORLD PROBLEMS IN THESE FIELDS.

6. **A FOCUS ON PRACTICAL APPLICATIONS**
   THROUGHOUT THE BOOK, THE EMPHASIS IS ON PRACTICAL, HANDS-ON EXPERIENCE. BY THE END OF THE BOOK, YOU'LL HAVE BUILT A SOLID FOUNDATION IN MATLAB AND BE READY TO TACKLE PROJECTS IN YOUR FIELD OF INTEREST, WHETHER THAT INVOLVES DATA ANALYSIS, MODELING, OR SIMULATIONS.

BOOK TITLE:

"MATLAB PROGRAMMING: A COMPREHENSIVE GUIDE FOR BEGINNERS"

TABLE OF CONTENTS

ABOUT THE AUTHOR

ANSHUMAN MISHRA, AN ACCOMPLISHED ACADEMIC AND EDUCATOR, HAS OVER 18 YEARS OF TEACHING EXPERIENCE AS AN ASSISTANT PROFESSOR IN COMPUTER SCIENCE. HE HOLDS AN M.TECH IN COMPUTER SCIENCE FROM THE PRESTIGIOUS BIRLA INSTITUTE OF TECHNOLOGY, MESRA. CURRENTLY SERVING AT DORANDA COLLEGE, RANCHI, HE SPECIALIZES IN PROGRAMMING LANGUAGES, SOFTWARE DEVELOPMENT, AND COMPUTER SKILLS, INSPIRING COUNTLESS STUDENTS WITH HIS PROFOUND KNOWLEDGE AND PRACTICAL INSIGHTS.

ANSHUMAN IS A PASSIONATE WRITER WITH EXPERTISE IN CREATING EDUCATIONAL RESOURCES FOR STUDENTS AND PROFESSIONALS. HIS BOOKS COVER TOPICS LIKE JAVA PROGRAMMING, SQL, OPERATING SYSTEMS, AND COMPETITIVE PROGRAMMING, REFLECTING HIS DEDICATION TO MAKING COMPLEX SUBJECTS ACCESSIBLE AND ENGAGING.

BEYOND ACADEMICS, ANSHUMAN IS A MOTIVATIONAL THINKER, A LOVER OF MYSTERIES, AND A STORYTELLER AT HEART. HE HAS AUTHORED WORKS RANGING FROM SELF-MOTIVATION GUIDES TO CHILDREN'S STORIES AND BOOKS DELVING INTO THE RICH HISTORY AND CULTURE OF JHARKHAND. HIS ABILITY TO WEAVE KNOWLEDGE WITH INSPIRATION MAKES HIS BOOKS A TREASURE FOR READERS OF ALL AGES.

"Programs must be written for people to read, and only incidentally for machines to execute."
— Harold Abelson & Gerald Jay Sussman, *Structure and Interpretation of Computer Programs*

Copyright Page

Title: **MATLAB PROGRAMMING: A COMPREHENSIVE GUIDE FOR BEGINNERS**

Author: Anshuman Kumar Mishra
Copyright © 2025 by Anshuman Kumar Mishra

This book is published for educational purposes and is intended to serve as a comprehensive guide for MCA and BCA students, educators, and aspiring programmers. The author has made every effort to ensure accuracy, but neither the author nor the publisher assumes responsibility for errors, omissions, or any consequences arising from the application of information in this book.

HOW TO STUDY THIS BOOK:

1. **START WITH THE BASICS:** BEGIN BY READING CHAPTER 1 AND CHAPTER 2, WHICH COVER THE INTRODUCTION TO PROGRAMMING AND MATLAB. THESE CHAPTERS WILL HELP YOU GET COMFORTABLE WITH THE MATLAB INTERFACE AND ITS SYNTAX. IF YOU'RE ALREADY FAMILIAR WITH C, YOU'LL FIND MANY OF THE CONCEPTS FAMILIAR, BUT TAKE YOUR TIME TO UNDERSTAND HOW THEY ARE IMPLEMENTED IN MATLAB.

2. **WORK THROUGH EXAMPLES AND EXERCISES:** AS YOU GO THROUGH EACH CHAPTER, MAKE SURE TO WORK THROUGH THE EXAMPLES PROVIDED. TRY TO UNDERSTAND THE REASONING BEHIND EACH STEP AND HOW IT TRANSLATES INTO MATLAB CODE. AFTER THAT, TACKLE THE EXERCISES AT THE END OF EACH CHAPTER. THESE EXERCISES ARE CRITICAL TO REINFORCING WHAT YOU'VE LEARNED.

3. **COMPARE MATLAB WITH C:** TAKE ADVANTAGE OF THE COMPARISONS BETWEEN MATLAB AND C PROGRAMMING THROUGHOUT THE BOOK. FOR EACH TOPIC, REVIEW THE C CODE EXAMPLE AND THEN SEE HOW THE SAME FUNCTIONALITY IS IMPLEMENTED IN MATLAB. THIS WILL HELP YOU UNDERSTAND THE DIFFERENCES IN SYNTAX AND FUNCTIONALITY, AND HIGHLIGHT THE STRENGTHS OF MATLAB IN VARIOUS AREAS, SUCH AS ARRAY MANIPULATION AND BUILT-IN FUNCTIONS.

4. **MAKE USE OF CASE STUDIES:** THE REAL-WORLD CASE STUDIES IN CHAPTER 10 PROVIDE EXCELLENT OPPORTUNITIES TO SEE HOW MATLAB CAN BE USED TO SOLVE PRACTICAL PROBLEMS. TRY TO REPLICATE THE EXAMPLES ON YOUR OWN AND EXPERIMENT WITH VARIATIONS OF THE CASE STUDIES. THIS WILL HELP YOU BECOME MORE CONFIDENT IN APPLYING MATLAB TO REAL-WORLD TASKS.

5. **USE MATLAB'S DOCUMENTATION AND RESOURCES:** AS YOU PROGRESS, DON'T HESITATE TO REFER TO MATLAB'S OFFICIAL DOCUMENTATION FOR MORE DETAILED INFORMATION ABOUT SPECIFIC FUNCTIONS OR TOOLBOXES. THE BOOK PROVIDES A FOUNDATION, BUT THE MATLAB DOCUMENTATION WILL BE AN INVALUABLE RESOURCE AS YOU CONTINUE LEARNING.

6. **REVIEW AND REINFORCE LEARNING:** AFTER COMPLETING A CHAPTER, TAKE A MOMENT TO REVIEW THE MATERIAL. REVISIT COMPLEX TOPICS AND PRACTICE WRITING CODE WITHOUT LOOKING AT THE EXAMPLES. THIS WILL SOLIDIFY YOUR UNDERSTANDING AND HELP YOU BECOME MORE PROFICIENT IN MATLAB PROGRAMMING.

7. **STUDY REGULARLY:** CONSISTENT STUDY AND PRACTICE ARE KEY TO MASTERING MATLAB. TRY TO SET ASIDE DEDICATED TIME EACH DAY TO GO THROUGH THE MATERIAL, EXPERIMENT WITH CODE, AND SOLVE EXERCISES.

OVER TIME, YOU'LL BUILD UP YOUR PROGRAMMING SKILLS AND BE ABLE TO APPLY THEM TO MORE ADVANCED TOPICS.

BY FOLLOWING THESE STEPS, YOU WILL NOT ONLY BECOME PROFICIENT IN MATLAB PROGRAMMING BUT ALSO DEEPEN YOUR UNDERSTANDING OF C PROGRAMMING CONCEPTS, ALLOWING YOU TO BE MORE VERSATILE IN YOUR PROGRAMMING CAREER.

CHAPTER 1: INTRODUCTION TO PROGRAMMING AND COMPUTERS

1.1 Components of a Computer

Hardware and Software Overview

Hardware refers to the physical components of a computer that are essential for its operation. These components are tangible and include:

- **CPU (Central Processing Unit):** Often referred to as the "brain" of the computer, the CPU performs all the processing tasks. It executes instructions from programs and performs calculations and logical operations. It is responsible for directing all the computer's activities and coordinating between other components.
- **Memory:** The computer's memory is crucial for temporarily storing data and instructions.
    - **RAM (Random Access Memory):** RAM is the computer's primary memory. It stores data that is actively being used by the CPU. RAM is volatile, meaning its contents are lost when the computer is turned off.
    - **ROM (Read-Only Memory):** ROM is non-volatile memory used to store critical instructions, such as the computer's BIOS, which helps start the system when powered on.
- **Storage Devices:** These include hard drives (HDDs), solid-state drives (SSDs), and optical drives (CD/DVD). Storage devices are used to permanently store data and programs.
- **I/O Devices (Input/Output Devices):** These allow the computer to interact with the user and other systems. Input devices like keyboards and mice allow the user to provide data to the computer, while output devices like monitors and printers allow the computer to display or print results.

On the other hand, **Software** refers to the programs and applications that run on the hardware. Software is responsible for telling the hardware what to do. Software can be classified into two main categories:

- **System Software:** This includes operating systems (like Windows, Linux, macOS), which manage hardware resources and provide an interface between hardware and user applications.
- **Application Software:** This includes programs like word processors, web browsers, or specialized tools such as MATLAB or C compilers. These programs enable the user to perform specific tasks on the computer.

Software essentially makes the hardware functional by providing it with instructions on how to process, store, and output data. It can either be compiled (like C programs) or interpreted (like MATLAB scripts).

Example: A Simple C Program

Let's consider a simple C program to print a message. While the program is written in C (software), it will run on physical hardware. The C compiler and the operating system are responsible for translating this software into machine code that the CPU can execute.

Here is an example in **C**:

```c
#include <stdio.h>

int main() {
    printf("Hello, World!\n");   // Message output to the monitor (I/O device)
    return 0;                    // Program ends successfully
}
```

- **Compilation Process:** The C program will be translated by a **C compiler** into machine code. The **compiler** takes the human-readable C code and converts it into binary instructions that the **CPU** can understand and execute.
- **Execution on Hardware:** The program will be executed by the CPU, and the message `"Hello, World!"` will be displayed on the monitor (output device). The computer's **RAM** will temporarily store the program and the values being used (like the string), and the **CPU** will process the instruction to send the result to the monitor.

The Role of the CPU, Memory, and I/O Devices

Each of these components plays a crucial role in making a computer function effectively:

- **CPU (Central Processing Unit):**
  The CPU is often referred to as the "brain" of the computer. It is responsible for interpreting and executing instructions from the software. The CPU performs operations like arithmetic (e.g., addition, subtraction) and logical (e.g., comparisons) computations. It also coordinates data transfer between different parts of the computer system, ensuring smooth operation.

  The CPU typically has several cores (processing units) to perform multiple tasks simultaneously. The CPU interacts with **memory** and **I/O devices** to process data and produce results.

- **Memory (RAM and ROM):**
  RAM (Random Access Memory) is the temporary working memory that stores data the CPU needs to access quickly during the execution of programs. The data in RAM is volatile, meaning that it is erased when the power is turned off. Programs, such as the simple C program we saw earlier, use RAM to store variables and other runtime data.

ROM (Read-Only Memory) is non-volatile and stores crucial instructions needed for starting up the computer. For instance, the BIOS (Basic Input/Output System) is stored in ROM and is essential for initializing hardware components during the boot process.

- **I/O Devices (Input/Output Devices):**
  I/O devices enable interaction between the computer and the external world. These include input devices like **keyboards** and **mice**, and output devices like **monitors** and **printers**. The **keyboard** sends input data to the CPU, and the **monitor** displays the results of processing. Other devices like printers and speakers also serve as output devices, allowing the computer to communicate results to users.

Example:

```
#include <stdio.h>

int main() {
    int num = 10;   // Variable stored in RAM
    printf("The number is: %d\n", num);   // Output to monitor (I/O device)
    return 0;
}
```

In this program:

- The **variable num** is stored in **RAM** because it's needed for the program's execution.
- The program's output (The number is: 10) will be sent to the **monitor** (an output I/O device) through the **CPU**.

Thus, in this simple program, we see how the **CPU** processes data, how **RAM** stores the variable, and how the result is displayed on an **I/O device** (the monitor).

1.2 Machine Code and Software Hierarchy

From High-Level Languages to Machine Code

High-level programming languages like **C** and **MATLAB** are designed to be human-readable and abstract away the complexities of low-level operations that occur at the hardware level. These languages allow programmers to focus on logic and problem-solving without needing to manually handle hardware interactions. However, the computer itself only understands **machine code**, which is a set of binary instructions (0s and 1s) that the **CPU** can execute.

To transform the high-level code into something the CPU can understand, a series of steps take place:

1. **Source Code (C or MATLAB)**:
   - This is the code you write as a programmer, using a high-level language like **C** or **MATLAB**. It's human-readable, so you can express complex ideas without having to deal with the intricacies of the computer's hardware.
2. **Compiler**:
   - A **compiler** takes the entire program written in a high-level language (like C or MATLAB) and translates it into an intermediate or assembly language. This step converts the source code into something that is more closely related to machine instructions but still not quite at the machine level.
3. **Assembler**:
   - After the code is translated by the compiler into **assembly language**, an **assembler** converts the assembly code into machine code. Assembly language is low-level and closely represents the actual binary instructions the CPU can understand, but it still uses human-readable mnemonics to represent machine instructions (like MOV for moving data, ADD for addition, etc.).
4. **Executable Code**:
   - Finally, the **executable code** is produced. This is the machine code (binary instructions) that the CPU can execute directly. The executable code is stored as a binary file (such as .exe on Windows or an executable file on Linux/macOS), and once the program is compiled and linked, the operating system can load this machine code into memory for execution.

Here's a breakdown of the process:

- **Source Code** (C or MATLAB) → **Compiler** → **Assembly Code** → **Assembler** → **Machine Code** (Executable)

Example: C Program Compilation Process

Let's take a simple C program as an example:

```
#include <stdio.h>

int main() {
    printf("Hello, World!\n");  // Print message to the console
    return 0;  // Exit the program successfully
}
```

1. **Source Code (C)**: This is the C code written by the programmer.
2. **Compiler**: The C compiler (like GCC) reads the source code and translates it into **assembly language** or an intermediate form. For instance, the compiler might output assembly code that looks something like this:

```
; Assembly code equivalent to the C program
SECTION .data
msg db 'Hello, World!',0   ; The message to be printed

SECTION .text
global _start
```

```
_start:
    ; Print the message
    mov eax, 4          ; System call number for write
    mov ebx, 1          ; File descriptor 1 (stdout)
    mov ecx, msg        ; Pointer to the message
    mov edx, 13         ; Message length
    int 0x80            ; Interrupt to make the system call

    ; Exit the program
    mov eax, 1          ; System call number for exit
    xor ebx, ebx        ; Return code 0
    int 0x80            ; Interrupt to exit the program
```

3. **Assembler**: The **assembler** takes this assembly code and converts it into machine code (binary form). The machine code would look something like:

```
10110000 11010000 11010100 .... (binary machine instructions)
```

4. **Executable Code**: The final **executable code** consists of binary instructions. The operating system loads this code into memory and the CPU executes it, displaying "Hello, World!" on the screen.

Compilers, Interpreters, and Assemblers

The process of translating high-level code into machine code can involve different tools depending on the language. The main tools involved are **compilers**, **interpreters**, and **assemblers**.

Compiler

A **compiler** is a program that takes the entire source code of a high-level language (like **C**) and translates it into machine code (binary instructions) before execution. The compiler does this in one go, creating an executable file that can be run independently without the need for the compiler. Once the source code is compiled, you can execute the program multiple times without needing to recompile.

For example, the **GCC (GNU Compiler Collection)** is a popular C compiler that converts C programs into machine code.

- **Advantages of Compilers:**
  - **Efficiency**: Since the program is compiled into machine code before running, the program executes faster.
  - **Portability**: The compiled machine code can be transferred and run on any compatible system without needing the source code or compiler.

Example: Here's a simple C program that would be compiled using a C compiler like GCC:

```
#include <stdio.h>

int main() {
    printf("Hello from the Compiler!\n");
    return 0;
}
```

- The **C compiler** translates this into machine code, producing an executable file that can run on the operating system. The program would be executed directly by the CPU.

Interpreter

An **interpreter** works differently from a compiler. It translates and executes the program **line-by-line** at runtime. It does not produce an executable file. Instead, it reads the high-level code, converts it to machine code on the fly, and immediately executes it.

Examples of interpreted languages include **MATLAB** and **Python**. These languages don't require a separate compilation step. The interpreter reads and executes the code line by line.

- **Advantages of Interpreters:**
  - **Ease of Debugging**: Since the code is executed line by line, it's easier to test and debug in real time.
  - **Portability**: The same source code can be run on any system with the interpreter installed.

Example: If you run a MATLAB script, the **MATLAB interpreter** processes and executes the commands as it reads them. If you write the following MATLAB code:

```
disp('Hello from the Interpreter!');
```

The interpreter will read the command, process it, and display the message in the command window.

Assembler

An **assembler** is a tool that converts **assembly language** (which is very close to machine code) into actual machine code. Assembly language uses mnemonic codes (like MOV, ADD, SUB) to represent low-level operations, which are easier for humans to read than raw machine code (binary).

After writing code in assembly language, you use an assembler to generate the corresponding machine code. Assemblers typically generate object files, which can then be linked into an executable.

Example: Here's an assembly program that prints a message to the screen in Linux:

```
section .data
    msg db 'Hello from the Assembler!', 0

section .text
    global _start

_start:
    ; Write message to stdout
    mov eax, 4          ; sys_write system call
    mov ebx, 1          ; file descriptor (1 is stdout)
    mov ecx, msg        ; pointer to the message
    mov edx, 22         ; length of the message
    int 0x80            ; call kernel

    ; Exit the program
    mov eax, 1          ; sys_exit system call
    xor ebx, ebx        ; exit code 0
    int 0x80            ; call kernel
```

After assembling this code, the assembler produces machine code (binary instructions) that the CPU can execute.

Summary of Key Concepts

1. **Machine Code**:
   - o The binary instructions (0s and 1s) that the CPU understands and executes. It's the final product of the translation process from high-level languages.
2. **Compilation Process**:
   - o **Source Code (C, MATLAB) → Compiler → Assembly Code → Assembler → Machine Code** (Executable).
3. **Compiler**:
   - o Translates the entire high-level program into machine code before execution. Once compiled, the program can run independently of the compiler.
4. **Interpreter**:
   - o Translates and executes high-level code line-by-line during runtime. There's no need for a separate compilation step.
5. **Assembler**:
   - o Converts assembly language (which is close to machine code) into binary machine code that the CPU can execute.

1.3 Working with Numbers

Number Systems: Binary, Decimal, Hexadecimal

In computing, numbers can be represented using different **number systems** or **bases**, depending on the requirements of the system. The three most commonly used number systems are:

1. **Binary (Base-2)**:
   - Binary is the most fundamental number system used by computers. It uses only two digits, **0** and **1**, to represent values. Each digit in a binary number is referred to as a **bit** (short for binary digit). All data in a computer, including numbers, text, and instructions, is ultimately represented in binary.
   - The binary system is well-suited for computers because digital circuits (transistors) can easily represent two states (on and off), which correspond to 1 and 0, respectively.
2. **Decimal (Base-10)**:
   - The decimal system is the number system most commonly used by humans in daily life. It uses **ten digits** (0-9). This is a **base-10** system, meaning each position represents a power of 10. For example, the number 256 in decimal is equivalent to: $2 \times 10^2 + 5 \times 10^1 + 6 \times 10^0 = 256$ $2 \times 10^2 + 5 \times 10^1 + 6 \times 10^0 = 256$
3. **Hexadecimal (Base-16)**:
   - Hexadecimal is a shorthand for representing binary numbers. It uses **16 symbols**, 0-9 and A-F, where **A-F** represent values 10 to 15. Hexadecimal is often used in computing to simplify the representation of binary values, as each hexadecimal digit represents exactly four binary digits (bits). For example, the binary number `1111 1111` can be written as `FF` in hexadecimal.

Example in C: Printing Binary, Decimal, and Hexadecimal

In C, we can print numbers in different formats such as binary, decimal, and hexadecimal. However, note that **C does not natively support binary output** with the `%b` format specifier, but we can still print decimal and hexadecimal representations.

```c
#include <stdio.h>

int main() {
    int num = 255;

    // Print the number in different formats
    printf("Decimal: %d\n", num);          // Decimal representation
(base-10)
    printf("Hexadecimal: %X\n", num);       // Hexadecimal representation
(base-16)

    // Note: C does not directly support binary output with %b
    // You can manually convert to binary if needed.
```

```
    return 0;
}
```

Output:

```
Decimal: 255
Hexadecimal: FF
```

In practice, to print binary in C, you would need to manually convert the integer into its binary form or use third-party libraries that provide this functionality.

Data Types in C vs MATLAB

When working with numbers, different programming languages provide different data types to represent various kinds of values.

C Data Types:

C is a **statically typed** language, which means you must declare the data type of a variable before using it. Common data types in C include:

- **int**: Integer type, used for whole numbers (e.g., 1, 100, -50).
- **float**: Single-precision floating-point, used for decimal numbers (e.g., 3.14, -0.001).
- **double**: Double-precision floating-point, used for numbers requiring more precision than `float`.
- **char**: Character type, used to store a single character (e.g., 'A', 'b').
- **void**: Used for functions that do not return a value.

MATLAB Data Types:

MATLAB is a **dynamically typed** language, which means you don't have to declare the type of a variable explicitly. MATLAB automatically determines the type based on the value assigned to the variable. Some of the common data types in MATLAB include:

- **double**: Default data type for floating-point numbers in MATLAB (e.g., 3.14, -0.001).
- **int8, int16, int32, int64**: Integer types with different sizes.
- **char**: Used to represent characters or strings.

Example in C:

```
#include <stdio.h>

int main() {
    int integerVal = 10;      // Integer
    float floatVal = 3.14;    // Floating-point
    char charVal = 'A';       // Character
```

```
    printf("Integer: %d\n", integerVal);   // Print integer
    printf("Float: %.2f\n", floatVal);      // Print float with 2 decimal
places
    printf("Character: %c\n", charVal);   // Print character

    return 0;
}
```

Equivalent in MATLAB:

```
integerVal = 10;    % Integer
floatVal = 3.14;    % Floating-point number
charVal = 'A';      % Character

disp(integerVal);   % Display integer
disp(floatVal);     % Display float
disp(charVal);      % Display character
```

In C, you explicitly declare the data type of each variable. In MATLAB, however, variables are dynamically typed, meaning you don't need to declare the type beforehand.

Precision and Accuracy in Numbers

In computing, **precision** refers to the number of digits a variable can store or display, while **accuracy** refers to how close a stored or computed value is to the actual value.

Precision in Floating-Point Numbers:

- **Float**: In C, a `float` variable stores a single-precision floating-point number, which means it provides less precision compared to `double`.
- **Double**: A `double` variable in C stores a double-precision floating-point number, offering higher precision.

For example, a `float` may store only up to 6-7 significant digits, while a `double` can store up to 15-16 significant digits.

Overflow and Underflow:

- **Overflow** occurs when a number exceeds the maximum value that can be represented by the chosen data type.
- **Underflow** occurs when a number is too small to be represented by the chosen data type.

Example in C (Precision Difference between Float and Double):

```
#include <stdio.h>

int main() {
    float a = 1.123456789;   // Low precision
```

```
double b = 1.123456789; // High precision

printf("Float value: %.6f\n", a);  // Will round to 6 decimal places
printf("Double value: %.9f\n", b); // Will show higher precision

return 0;
}
```

Output:

```
Float value: 1.123457
Double value: 1.123456789
```

- In the output, the `float` value is rounded to 6 decimal places due to its lower precision, while the `double` maintains higher precision, showing more significant digits.

Introduction to Programming and Computers - MCQs

1.1 Components of a Computer

1. **Which of the following is considered hardware?** a) Operating System
   b) Compiler
   c) Keyboard
   d) C Program

   Answer: c) Keyboard

2. **What does software refer to in a computer system?** a) Physical devices like CPU and RAM
   b) Instructions and data used by hardware
   c) Input devices like the mouse
   d) The operating system only

   Answer: b) Instructions and data used by hardware

3. **Which of the following is the main function of the CPU?** a) Store data
   b) Perform arithmetic and logical operations
   c) Provide input and output functions
   d) Display results on the screen

   Answer: b) Perform arithmetic and logical operations

4. **RAM is used to store data that is:** a) Permanent and non-volatile
   b) Temporary and volatile
   c) Only used for input
   d) Only used for output

   Answer: b) Temporary and volatile

5. **Which of the following is an example of an I/O device?** a) CPU
   b) Hard Drive
   c) Monitor
   d) RAM

   Answer: c) Monitor

1.2 Machine Code and Software Hierarchy

6. **What is the main difference between high-level languages (e.g., C) and machine code?** a) High-level languages are harder for computers to understand
   b) High-level languages are written in binary
   c) Machine code is more human-readable
   d) High-level languages are designed for humans, while machine code is for the CPU

   Answer: d) High-level languages are designed for humans, while machine code is for the CPU

7. **Which of the following is responsible for translating high-level language into machine code?** a) Operating System
   b) Compiler
   c) Interpreter
   d) Assembler

   Answer: b) Compiler

8. **What does an assembler do?** a) Translates high-level code into assembly language
   b) Converts assembly language into machine code

c) Interprets high-level code during execution
d) Compiles C code into object code

Answer: b) Converts assembly language into machine code

---

9. **Which language is directly understood by the CPU?** a) Assembly language
   b) High-level programming languages
   c) Machine code
   d) Python

   Answer: c) Machine code

---

10. **Which of the following is an example of an interpreted language?** a) C
    b) Java
    c) MATLAB
    d) Assembly

Answer: c) MATLAB

---

11. **Which of the following is an advantage of using a compiler over an interpreter?** a) Compilers translate code line by line
    b) Compilers provide immediate output
    c) Compiled programs typically run faster
    d) Interpreters can handle errors better

Answer: c) Compiled programs typically run faster

---

12. **What is the main function of a compiler in the programming process?** a) It interprets the source code and executes it immediately
    b) It converts high-level source code into machine code
    c) It manages input and output for the program
    d) It stores the program for later execution

Answer: b) It converts high-level source code into machine code

---

13. **Which of the following tools is used to convert assembly code into machine code?** a) Compiler
    b) Interpreter
    c) Assembler
    d) Debugger

Answer: c) Assembler

---

14. **Which of the following is true regarding interpreters?** a) They compile the entire program into machine code before execution
    b) They execute code line-by-line at runtime
    c) They are faster than compilers
    d) They require the source code to be compiled first

Answer: b) They execute code line-by-line at runtime

1.3 Working with Numbers

15. **What is the base of the binary number system?** a) Base-10
    b) Base-2
    c) Base-16
    d) Base-8

Answer: b) Base-2

---

16. **Which number system uses digits 0-9 and letters A-F?** a) Decimal
    b) Binary
    c) Hexadecimal
    d) Octal

Answer: c) Hexadecimal

---

17. **What is the main advantage of using hexadecimal over binary?** a) Hexadecimal is easier for computers to process
    b) Hexadecimal numbers are more compact and easier to read than binary
    c) Binary numbers are longer to write than hexadecimal
    d) Hexadecimal numbers take up less memory than binary

Answer: b) Hexadecimal numbers are more compact and easier to read than binary

18. **Which of the following C format specifiers is used to print an integer in hexadecimal?** a) `%d`
    b) `%f`
    c) `%X`
    d) `%b`

Answer: c) `%X`

19. **Which of the following is not a valid data type in C?** a) `int`
    b) `float`
    c) `double`
    d) `string`

Answer: d) `string` (C uses `char[]` or `char*` for strings, not `string` type)

20. **In C, which of the following is used to store a single character?** a) `char`
    b) `int`
    c) `float`
    d) `string`

Answer: a) `char`

21. **Which data type in C would be best suited for storing a number like 3.14159?** a) `int`
    b) `char`
    c) `float`
    d) `double`

Answer: d) `double`

22. **In MATLAB, which data type is used by default for numbers with decimal points?**
    a) `int`
    b) `double`
    c) `float`
    d) `char`

Answer: b) `double`

---

23. **In C, what happens when a floating-point number exceeds the maximum value that can be represented by its data type?** a) It causes an error
b) It results in overflow
c) It is automatically converted to a double
d) The program will terminate immediately

Answer: b) It results in overflow

---

24. **Which of the following describes the concept of "precision" in floating-point numbers?** a) How accurate the number is to the actual value
b) The number of digits a number can store
c) The maximum possible value the number can represent
d) The number of decimal places the number has

Answer: b) The number of digits a number can store

---

25. **Which of the following is the primary difference between the `float` and `double` data types in C?** a) `float` is used for whole numbers, and `double` is used for decimal numbers
b) `double` provides higher precision than `float`
c) `double` is used for storing characters, and `float` is used for numbers
d) There is no difference between `float` and `double`

Answer: b) `double` provides higher precision than `float`

1.1 Components of a Computer

Question 1:

Write a C program that prints the components of a computer (Hardware vs Software) and explains them.

Answer:

```c
#include <stdio.h>
int main() {
    printf("Hardware Components:\n");
    printf("- CPU: The brain of the computer, performs calculations.\n");
```

```
    printf("- Memory: Temporary storage for data and instructions.\n");
    printf("- Storage Devices: Hard drives, SSDs, store data
permanently.\n");
    printf("- I/O Devices: Input devices (keyboard, mouse) and output devices
(monitor).\n");

    printf("\nSoftware Components:\n");
    printf("- Operating System: Manages hardware and software resources.\n");
    printf("- Applications: Programs like word processors, compilers,
etc.\n");

    return 0;
}
```

Question 2:

Write a C program that simulates the interaction between the CPU and memory by storing and retrieving data from memory.

Answer:

```
#include <stdio.h>

int main() {
    int memoryLocation;   // Memory in CPU

    // CPU stores data in memory
    memoryLocation = 100;

    // CPU retrieves data from memory
    printf("Data stored in memory: %d\n", memoryLocation);

    return 0;
}
```

1.2 Machine Code and Software Hierarchy

Question 3:

Write a C program that demonstrates the use of high-level languages (C code) being compiled into machine code. The program itself doesn't show the machine code, but it highlights how a simple task can be done using C.

Answer:

```
#include <stdio.h>

int main() {
    printf("This is a simple C program that will eventually be compiled into
machine code.\n");
```

```
        return 0;
}
```

Explanation: This program demonstrates a simple task (printing a message) written in C. When this program is compiled, the C code is converted into machine code that the CPU can execute. This is done by the compiler.

Question 4:

Write a C program that demonstrates a basic `if` statement, which would be interpreted by the compiler into machine code.

Answer:

```c
#include <stdio.h>

int main() {
    int number = 10;

    if (number > 5) {
        printf("The number is greater than 5.\n");
    } else {
        printf("The number is not greater than 5.\n");
    }

    return 0;
}
```

Explanation: The `if` condition is written in C, and when compiled, it will be translated into machine code instructions that the CPU can execute.

1.3 Working with Numbers

Question 5:

Write a C program to convert a decimal number to binary.

Answer:

```c
#include <stdio.h>

void decimalToBinary(int n) {
    if (n > 1) {
        decimalToBinary(n / 2);
    }
    printf("%d", n % 2);
```

```
}

int main() {
    int number;
    printf("Enter a decimal number: ");
    scanf("%d", &number);
    printf("Binary equivalent: ");
    decimalToBinary(number);
    printf("\n");

    return 0;
}
```

Explanation: This program recursively divides the number by 2 and prints the remainder, which represents the binary digits.

Question 6:

Write a C program to convert a hexadecimal number to decimal.

Answer:

```
#include <stdio.h>
#include <stdlib.h>

int main() {
    char hex[20];
    printf("Enter a hexadecimal number: ");
    scanf("%s", hex);

    // Convert hexadecimal to decimal
    int decimal = (int)strtol(hex, NULL, 16);

    printf("Decimal equivalent: %d\n", decimal);

    return 0;
}
```

Explanation: The strtol() function converts the hexadecimal input to its decimal equivalent.

Question 7:

Write a C program to print a number in binary, decimal, and hexadecimal formats.

Answer:

```
#include <stdio.h>

int main() {
    int num = 255;
```

```
    printf("Binary: ");
    for (int i = 31; i >= 0; i--) {
        printf("%d", (num >> i) & 1);
    }
    printf("\n");

    printf("Decimal: %d\n", num);
    printf("Hexadecimal: %X\n", num);

    return 0;
}
```

Explanation: The program first prints the number in binary by shifting the bits of the number. It also prints the decimal and hexadecimal formats using standard C format specifiers.

Question 8:

Write a C program to demonstrate the difference between `float` and `double` precision by displaying the same number with different data types.

Answer:

```
#include <stdio.h>

int main() {
    float a = 3.1415926535;
    double b = 3.1415926535;

    printf("Float: %.6f\n", a);   // Will show limited precision
    printf("Double: %.10f\n", b); // Shows more precision

    return 0;
}
```

Explanation: The program shows the difference in precision between `float` and `double` by printing a decimal number with different precision levels.

Question 9:

Write a C program to demonstrate integer overflow by assigning a value greater than the maximum limit of an `int`.

Answer:

```
#include <stdio.h>
#include <limits.h>
```

```
int main() {
    int num = INT_MAX;
    printf("Maximum value of int: %d\n", num);

    // Integer overflow
    num = num + 1;   // Overflow occurs here

    printf("Value after overflow: %d\n", num);

    return 0;
}
```

Explanation: This program shows how an integer can overflow when it exceeds the maximum value an `int` can store.

Question 10:

Write a C program that reads two numbers and calculates their sum, product, and difference, using `int` and `float` data types.

Answer:

```
#include <stdio.h>

int main() {
    int int1, int2;
    float float1, float2;

    printf("Enter two integers: ");
    scanf("%d %d", &int1, &int2);

    printf("Enter two floating-point numbers: ");
    scanf("%f %f", &float1, &float2);

    printf("Integer sum: %d\n", int1 + int2);
    printf("Integer product: %d\n", int1 * int2);
    printf("Integer difference: %d\n", int1 - int2);

    printf("Floating-point sum: %.2f\n", float1 + float2);
    printf("Floating-point product: %.2f\n", float1 * float2);
    printf("Floating-point difference: %.2f\n", float1 - float2);

    return 0;
}
```

Explanation: The program reads two integer and two floating-point values, and calculates their sum, product, and difference using both data types (`int` and `float`).

CHAPTER 2: GETTING STARTED WITH MATLAB

2.1 MATLAB Desktop: Command Window, Editor, and Workspace

MATLAB is an interactive computing environment that provides powerful tools for numerical computation, data analysis, visualization, and algorithm development. The MATLAB interface consists of several essential components that work together to facilitate a seamless user experience. These components include the **Command Window**, **Editor**, and **Workspace**.

---

1. Command Window

The **Command Window** is the central part of the MATLAB interface where you interact with the software. It is essentially a place where you can directly type and execute commands. Any expression or command you input into the Command Window is executed immediately, and MATLAB shows the results right after the command.

Key Features of the Command Window:

- **Interactive Command Input**: You can type mathematical expressions, assignments, or function calls directly into the Command Window.
- **Immediate Feedback**: MATLAB provides immediate feedback for most commands. For example, if you perform a simple calculation like 2 + 3, MATLAB will instantly return the result.
- **History and Reusability**: You can use the **up** and **down** arrow keys to navigate through previous commands in the history, making it easier to repeat or modify earlier commands.

Example:

When you type the command 2 + 3 into the Command Window, MATLAB immediately returns the result:

```
>> 2 + 3
ans =
    5
```

Here, the result 5 is displayed in the Command Window. The output variable ans is automatically assigned by MATLAB to hold the result of the expression.

---

2. Editor

The **Editor** is the place where you can write, edit, and save your MATLAB scripts and functions. Scripts and functions are saved in files with a .m extension, and these files can contain multiple lines of MATLAB code. The Editor is a sophisticated tool that helps you write MATLAB programs more efficiently, with features like:

- **Syntax Highlighting**: Different parts of the code, such as keywords, variables, functions, and comments, are color-coded to make the code easier to read and understand.
- **Error Checking**: MATLAB automatically checks for errors in the code while you are typing, helping you identify and fix issues before running the code.
- **Debugging**: The Editor provides debugging tools such as breakpoints, step-through execution, and variable inspection to help you troubleshoot and debug your code.
- **File Management**: You can open, save, and organize your MATLAB files within the Editor.

Example:

Here is a simple MATLAB script that adds two numbers and displays the result using the Editor:

```
% Simple MATLAB script
a = 5;
b = 3;
sum_ab = a + b;
disp(sum_ab);
```

- The script above defines two variables a and b, calculates their sum, and displays the result using $disp()$.
- You can save this script as a .m file (e.g., add_numbers.m), and later run it from the Editor or the Command Window.

3. Workspace

The **Workspace** is an essential component that displays all the variables currently stored in memory. It gives you an overview of your working variables, including their names, values, and sizes. The Workspace allows you to manage your variables and monitor their states during the execution of your code.

Key Features of the Workspace:

- **Variables Overview**: All the variables you define in the Command Window or Editor are listed in the Workspace, along with their values.
- **Interactive Management**: You can modify, delete, or inspect variables directly from the Workspace window.
- **Data Inspection**: You can double-click on a variable in the Workspace to open it in a variable editor, which helps you view more complex data structures, such as matrices or arrays.

Example:

When you define a variable in the Command Window, such as:

```
>> x = 10;
```

The Workspace will display the variable x with the value 10. In the Workspace, you can:

- Inspect the value of x,
- Modify it directly (if needed),
- Delete it if no longer needed.

If you define additional variables, they will also be added to the Workspace, and you can see their current values and properties.

Managing Files and Paths in MATLAB

MATLAB allows you to manage your code and files effectively by using a straightforward file system and path management system.

1. Managing Files

MATLAB files typically have a .m extension and can be either **scripts** or **functions**:

- **Scripts**: A script is a collection of MATLAB commands that are executed sequentially. It does not accept inputs or return outputs like a function. Scripts are often used for performing a series of operations or running a sequence of commands.
- **Functions**: A function is a more structured form of code that can accept inputs and return outputs. Functions in MATLAB are defined using the function keyword and can be stored in .m files.

To create or open a file in MATLAB:

- You can use the **Editor** to write new scripts or functions, and then save them to disk.
- You can open existing files via the file management toolbar or using the **Current Folder** window.

Example:

A script file (add_numbers.m) might look like this:

```
% add_numbers.m
a = 5;
b = 10;
result = a + b;
disp(result);
```

Once saved, you can run this script from the Command Window by typing its name (without the .m extension):

```
>> add_numbers
```

2. Paths in MATLAB

MATLAB uses a system of **paths** to locate the functions, scripts, and other files that you create or need. The MATLAB path determines which folders MATLAB searches for files when you call a function or script.

Default Path:

When you launch MATLAB, it automatically sets the default path to the current working directory (the folder you are working in) and includes directories from the MATLAB installation. However, you can add or remove directories from the path to ensure MATLAB can find your custom functions or scripts.

Adding and Removing Paths:

- You can add a folder to the MATLAB search path using the addpath function:

  ```
  addpath('C:\my_functions');
  ```

- You can remove a folder from the path using the rmpath function:

  ```
  rmpath('C:\my_functions');
  ```

- Alternatively, you can use the **pathtool** to view and modify the MATLAB search path through a graphical user interface. This tool allows you to easily manage your paths without typing commands.

Example:

If you have a folder C:\my_functions where you store your custom MATLAB functions, you can add it to the MATLAB path to ensure MATLAB can access those functions when needed. You can do this by either using the addpath function in the Command Window or by using the **pathtool**.

2.2 Writing Your First Program in MATLAB

In this section, we'll explore how to write your first MATLAB program, covering MATLAB's syntax and structure. We'll also discuss how simple C programs can be translated into MATLAB, helping you understand the differences and similarities between the two programming languages.

MATLAB Syntax and Structure

MATLAB syntax is designed to be intuitive and easy to understand, especially for mathematical and numerical operations. Below are some essential components of MATLAB's syntax and structure:

1. Comments

In MATLAB, comments are used to explain or annotate the code, making it easier to understand. Comments are ignored by MATLAB during execution, meaning they don't affect the program's behavior. To write comments in MATLAB, you use the percent symbol (%). Anything that follows the % symbol on a line is treated as a comment.

- **Single-line comment**: Use the % symbol to comment a single line.

```
% This is a comment
```

- **Multi-line comments**: You can use multiple % symbols for multi-line comments, or use %% to indicate block comments, commonly used to mark sections in the code.

```
% This is the first comment
% This is the second comment
%% This section of code does addition
```

2. Variables and Assignment

In MATLAB, variables do not need to be declared before they are used. MATLAB is dynamically typed, which means the type of the variable is automatically inferred based on the value assigned to it. Assignment of values to variables is done using the = operator.

- **Assigning an integer to a variable**:

```
x = 5;    % Assign 5 to variable x
```

- **Assigning a floating-point number to a variable**:

```
y = 3.14;    % Assign 3.14 to variable y
```

MATLAB automatically detects the data type, so there's no need for explicit data type declarations, as required in languages like C.

3. End of Lines

MATLAB does not require a semicolon at the end of a statement. However, if you include a semicolon at the end of a statement, it suppresses the output, preventing MATLAB from displaying the result in the Command Window.

- **Without a semicolon**: MATLAB will display the result in the Command Window.

```
x = 5    % This will display 'x = 5'
```

- **With a semicolon**: MATLAB will not display the result.

```
x = 5;   % No output will be shown
```

This feature is useful when writing scripts and functions where you want to control whether or not intermediate results are printed.

4. Vectors and Matrices

MATLAB is designed around matrix and vector operations. You can easily create vectors and matrices using square brackets ([ ]). Vectors can be either row vectors or column vectors, and matrices are represented as 2D arrays of numbers.

- **Creating a matrix**: A matrix in MATLAB is created by separating elements with commas or spaces for elements in the same row, and semicolons (;) to separate rows.

```
A = [1, 2, 3; 4, 5, 6];   % A 2x3 matrix
```

This creates a matrix A with two rows and three columns:

```
A =
     1     2     3
     4     5     6
```

- **Creating a column vector**:

```
B = [1; 2; 3];   % A 3x1 column vector
```

This creates a column vector B with three elements:

```
B =
     1
     2
     3
```

MATLAB's ability to handle vectors and matrices as first-class data types makes it particularly powerful for numerical computations.

Translating Simple C Programs to MATLAB

To help understand how MATLAB works compared to C, let's look at how simple programs written in C can be translated into MATLAB code. We'll begin with an example of adding two numbers.

C Program Example (Adding Two Numbers)

In C, you would write a program like this:

```c
#include <stdio.h>

int main() {
    int a = 5, b = 10;
    int sum = a + b;
    printf("The sum is: %d\n", sum);
    return 0;
}
```

- **Explanation of C Code:**
  - The `#include <stdio.h>` line includes the standard input-output library.
  - `int a = 5, b = 10;` declares two integer variables and initializes them.
  - `int sum = a + b;` calculates the sum of `a` and `b` and stores it in the `sum` variable.
  - The `printf()` function is used to display the result.

MATLAB Equivalent

In MATLAB, the equivalent program to add two numbers would look like this:

```matlab
% Simple addition in MATLAB
a = 5;          % Assign 5 to a
b = 10;         % Assign 10 to b
sum = a + b;    % Add a and b
disp(['The sum is: ', num2str(sum)]);   % Display the result as a string
```

- **Explanation of MATLAB Code:**
  - The `%` symbol is used for a comment explaining the code.
  - `a = 5;` and `b = 10;` assign values to the variables `a` and `b`.
  - `sum = a + b;` calculates the sum of `a` and `b` and stores it in the variable `sum`.
  - `disp(['The sum is: ', num2str(sum)]);` is used to display the sum. `disp()` is a MATLAB function that prints to the Command Window. `num2str(sum)` converts the numeric value of `sum` into a string so it can be concatenated with the message.

Key Differences Between C and MATLAB

1. **Variable Declaration**:
    - In C, variables must be declared with their types before use (`int a;`).
    - In MATLAB, there is no need to declare variables; MATLAB infers their type based on the assigned value.
2. **Displaying Output**:
    - In C, `printf()` is used to display output.
    - In MATLAB, `disp()` is used for simple output, and `num2str()` is often used to convert numbers into strings for display.
3. **Semicolons**:
    - In C, semicolons are required to end each statement.
    - In MATLAB, semicolons are optional but used to suppress output.
4. **Functions and Scripts**:
    - C requires a `main()` function to execute the program.
    - MATLAB does not require a `main()` function. Instead, you can write scripts or functions that execute directly from the Command Window or Editor.

2.3 Expressions and Variables

In this section, we'll go over how to define and use variables and constants in MATLAB, how assignment and operators work, and how data types are handled. Understanding these fundamentals will help you write clean and efficient code in MATLAB.

Defining Constants and Variables

1. Variables in MATLAB

In MATLAB, variables are very flexible and do not require explicit declaration of their data types, unlike in languages like C. You simply assign a value to a variable, and MATLAB automatically determines the variable's type based on the assigned value. This dynamic typing makes MATLAB easy to use for mathematical and numerical computations.

For example:

```
a = 5;      % Integer assignment
b = 3.14;   % Floating-point assignment
```

Here:

- `a` is automatically treated as an integer.
- `b` is treated as a floating-point number.

MATLAB can work with these variables without you needing to define their type explicitly beforehand.

2. Constants in MATLAB

While MATLAB does not have a built-in constant declaration like some other programming languages (e.g., `const` in C), you can simulate constants by following a naming convention. By convention, constants in MATLAB are typically written in uppercase letters, and you should avoid reassigning them after their initial definition.

For example:

```
PI = 3.14159;   % Define a constant value for Pi
```

Here, `PI` is defined as a constant, and even though MATLAB will not enforce immutability, the convention of using uppercase letters signals to other programmers that this value should not be changed.

Assignment Statements and Operator Use in MATLAB vs C

1. Assignment in MATLAB and C

In both MATLAB and C, the = symbol is used for assignment. However, there are key differences between how assignment works in these two languages:

- **In C**, variables must be declared with a specific type before you assign a value to them. This requires specifying the type of the variable (e.g., `int`, `float`, `char`).

  For example:

  ```c
  Copy
  int x = 5;   // Declare x as an integer and assign it the value 5
  ```

- **In MATLAB**, you don't need to declare the type of a variable. MATLAB infers the type based on the assigned value. You just assign the value to the variable directly.

  For example:

  ```
  x = 5;   % MATLAB automatically treats x as an integer (or double in this case)
  ```

2. Arithmetic Operators

MATLAB supports a wide range of arithmetic operations, just like C. Common arithmetic operators include addition (+), subtraction (-), multiplication (*), and division (/). The syntax for these operations is the same in both languages, but MATLAB does not require variable type declaration before assignment.

For example:

```
a = 10;
b = 5;
sum_ab = a + b;   % Addition in MATLAB
```

In C, you would do the same, but with explicit type declarations:

```
#include <stdio.h>

int main() {
    int a = 10, b = 5;
    int sum_ab = a + b;   // Addition in C
    printf("Sum: %d", sum_ab);
    return 0;
}
```

As you can see, while the basic arithmetic syntax is the same, C requires type declarations, and MATLAB does not.

3. Relational and Logical Operators

MATLAB also supports relational operators like ==, >, <, and logical operators like && (AND) and || (OR), similar to C. These operators are used to compare values or test conditions.

For example, checking if two values are equal:

```
if a == b
    disp('a is equal to b');
end
```

This code in C would look similar:

```
if (a -- b) {
    printf("a is equal to b\n");
}
```

In both languages:

- == checks for equality.
- > and < check for greater than and less than.
- && and || are logical AND and OR operators.

Working with Data Types

1. Data Types in MATLAB

MATLAB supports several data types, and some of the most commonly used are:

- **Numeric types**:
  - `double` (default): Used for storing floating-point numbers.
  - `single`: Used for single-precision floating-point numbers.
  - `int8`, `int16`, `int32`, `int64`: Integer types of various sizes.
- **Character types**:
  - `char`: Used for single characters.
  - `string`: Used for text strings (introduced in MATLAB R2016b).
- **Logical**:
  - `logical`: Used to store Boolean values (true or false).

For example:

```
x = 5;          % Default type is double
y = single(5);  % Single precision
z = 'Hello';    % String
```

Here:

- `x` is a `double` (default type).
- `y` is explicitly declared as `single`.
- `z` is a string of characters (`char` type).

2. Type Conversion

MATLAB allows explicit type conversion using functions like `double()`, `int32()`, and `single()`. This is useful when you need to convert one type of data to another, such as when you need higher or lower precision or different representations of numbers.

For example:

```
x = int32(5);   % Convert 5 to an integer of 32-bit type
y = double(x);  % Convert x back to double precision
```

This can be useful when you need to handle data with specific precision requirements.

3. Matrices and Arrays

MATLAB is designed to work with matrices and arrays natively, and these are fundamental data structures in MATLAB. You can easily define matrices and arrays, and MATLAB provides powerful built-in functions for matrix manipulation. Operators like addition, subtraction, multiplication, and division apply directly to arrays and matrices.

For example:

```
A = [1, 2, 3; 4, 5, 6];  % A 2x3 matrix
B = [7, 8, 9; 10, 11, 12]; % Another 2x3 matrix
C = A + B; % Matrix addition
```

Here:

- A and B are matrices with two rows and three columns each.
- C is the result of adding the two matrices element-wise.

You can also perform operations like matrix multiplication:

```
D = A * B';  % Matrix multiplication (transpose B for correct dimensions)
```

MATLAB handles all these operations with ease and is especially suited for numerical and scientific computing tasks that involve matrix manipulations.

---

25 multiple-choice questions (MCQs) :

2.1 Introduction to MATLAB Interface

1. **What is the primary purpose of the Command Window in MATLAB?**
   - A) To write and save scripts
   - B) To display results and execute commands interactively
   - C) To manage file paths
   - D) To create plots and graphs
   - **Answer**: B) To display results and execute commands interactively
2. **Which of the following is NOT typically found in the MATLAB Desktop?**
   - A) Command Window
   - B) Editor
   - C) Workspace
   - D) Java Console
   - **Answer**: D) Java Console
3. **What type of file extension do MATLAB scripts have?**
   - A) .txt
   - B) .mat
   - C) .m
   - D) .ml
   - **Answer**: C) .m
4. **In MATLAB, which window shows all the variables currently in the memory?**
   - A) Command Window
   - B) Editor
   - C) Workspace
   - D) History
   - **Answer**: C) Workspace
5. **Which command is used to add a folder to the MATLAB path?**

- o A) addpath()
- o B) setpath()
- o C) newfolder()
- o D) folderadd()
- o **Answer**: A) addpath()

6. **In MATLAB, which button would you use to run a script from the editor?**
   - o A) Execute
   - o B) Start
   - o C) Run
   - o D) Play
   - o **Answer**: C) Run

7. **Where do you enter MATLAB commands for immediate execution?**
   - o A) Editor
   - o B) Command Window
   - o C) Workspace
   - o D) File Manager
   - o **Answer**: B) Command Window

8. **Which of the following is a key feature of the MATLAB Editor?**
   - o A) It only runs pre-written code
   - o B) It cannot debug MATLAB code
   - o C) It supports syntax highlighting and error checking
   - o D) It only runs mathematical functions
   - o **Answer**: C) It supports syntax highlighting and error checking

9. **Which function is used to display the current working directory in MATLAB?**
   - o A) cd()
   - o B) dir()
   - o C) pwd()
   - o D) ls()
   - o **Answer**: C) pwd()

10. **How do you remove a folder from the MATLAB search path?**
    - o A) deletepath()
    - o B) rmpath()
    - o C) remfolder()
    - o D) removepath()
    - o **Answer**: B) rmpath()

2.2 Writing Your First Program in MATLAB

11. **In MATLAB, which symbol is used to start a comment?**
    - o A) #
    - o B) //
    - o C) --
    - o D) %
    - o **Answer**: D) %

12. **Which of the following is the correct syntax for assigning the value 5 to a variable x in MATLAB?**
    - A) x := 5
    - B) x = 5;
    - C) let x = 5;
    - D) x <- 5
    - **Answer:** B) x = 5;
13. **How do you display the value of a variable in MATLAB?**
    - A) show(x)
    - B) print(x)
    - C) disp(x)
    - D) output(x)
    - **Answer:** C) disp(x)
14. **Which of the following is NOT a valid MATLAB variable name?**
    - A) myVar
    - B) _myVar
    - C) 2ndVar
    - D) my_var
    - **Answer:** C) 2ndVar
15. **In MATLAB, how would you write a simple script that adds two numbers, 5 and 10, and displays the result?**
    - A) sum = 5 + 10; disp(sum);
    - B) sum = 5 + 10; print(sum);
    - C) sum = 5 + 10; display(sum);
    - D) disp(5 + 10);
    - **Answer:** A) sum = 5 + 10; disp(sum);
16. **Which of the following is the correct way to save a MATLAB script?**
    - A) File -> Save As -> MyScript.m
    - B) File -> Save -> script.m
    - C) Save -> script
    - D) File -> Export -> Save As script.m
    - **Answer:** A) File -> Save As -> MyScript.m
17. **Which of the following best describes the MATLAB language?**
    - A) Assembly Language
    - B) High-Level Programming Language
    - C) Machine Code
    - D) Markup Language
    - **Answer:** B) High-Level Programming Language
18. **How would you assign the value 3.14 to a variable pi in MATLAB?**
    - A) pi = 3.14;
    - B) Pi := 3.14;
    - C) pi = '3.14';
    - D) 3.14 -> pi;
    - **Answer:** A) pi = 3.14;
19. **What does the MATLAB function num2str() do?**
    - A) Converts a string to a number

- o B) Converts a number to a string
- o C) Converts a matrix to a string
- o D) Changes the number of decimal points
- o **Answer**: B) Converts a number to a string
20. **Which of the following would display the sum of variables a and b in MATLAB?**
    - o A) disp(a + b);
    - o B) display(a + b);
    - o C) output(a + b);
    - o D) print(a + b);
    - o **Answer**: A) disp(a + b);

2.3 Expressions and Variables

21. **How do you define a constant in MATLAB?**
    - o A) By using the const keyword
    - o B) By using uppercase letters and not reassigning the value
    - o C) By using the `constant` keyword
    - o D) Constants are not supported in MATLAB
    - o **Answer**: B) By using uppercase letters and not reassigning the value
22. **Which of the following statements correctly assigns an integer value to a variable in MATLAB?**
    - o A) int x = 5;
    - o B) x = int(5);
    - o C) x = 5;
    - o D) x = integer(5);
    - o **Answer**: C) x = 5;
23. **Which operator is used for matrix multiplication in MATLAB?**
    - o A) *
    - o B) .*
    - o C) **
    - o D) x*
    - o **Answer**: A) *
24. **Which of the following operators are used for logical AND and OR in MATLAB?**
    - o A) && and ||
    - o B) AND and OR
    - o C) & and |
    - o D) AND and OR are not supported
    - o **Answer**: A) && and ||
25. **Which MATLAB function is used to convert an integer to a double precision value?**
    - o A) toDouble()
    - o B) int2double()
    - o C) double()
    - o D) cast()
    - o **Answer**: C) double()

2.1 Introduction to MATLAB Interface

1. **Question:** What will happen if you run the following command in the MATLAB Command Window?

   ```
   x = 5;
   ```

   Answer: The variable x will be assigned the value 5, and the result will be stored in the MATLAB workspace. No output will be shown because the statement ends with a semicolon.

2. **Question:** How would you open the Editor to write a script in MATLAB? **Answer:** To open the Editor, click on the **New Script** button in the MATLAB desktop or type edit in the Command Window and press Enter.

3. **Question:** How can you check which files are currently in the MATLAB workspace? **Answer:** You can view the current variables in the workspace by looking at the **Workspace** panel in the MATLAB desktop. You can also use the who or whos command in the Command Window.

4. **Question:** Write a command to add the directory C:\myFunctions to the MATLAB search path. **Answer:**

   ```
   addpath('C:\myFunctions');
   ```

5. **Question:** If you want to remove the folder C:\myFunctions from the MATLAB search path, which command would you use? **Answer:**

   ```
   rmpath('C:\myFunctions');
   ```

2.2 Writing Your First Program in MATLAB

6. **Question:** Write a simple MATLAB program that calculates the sum of two numbers (5 and 10) and displays the result. **Answer:**

   ```
   a = 5;
   b = 10;
   sum_ab = a + b;
   disp(['The sum is: ', num2str(sum_ab)]);
   ```

7. **Question:** What is the output of the following MATLAB code?

   ```
   x = 10;
   y = 2;
   disp(x / y);
   ```

   Answer: The output will be:

   ```
   5
   ```

8. **Question:** Translate the following C code into MATLAB:

```c
int x = 5;
int y = 10;
printf("The sum is: %d", x + y);
```

Answer:

```matlab
x = 5;
y = 10;
disp(['The sum is: ', num2str(x + y)]);
```

9. **Question:** Write a MATLAB program to calculate the area of a circle with radius 4. Use the formula `Area = pi * r^2`. **Answer:**

```matlab
r = 4;
Area = pi * r^2;
disp(['The area of the circle is: ', num2str(Area)]);
```

10. **Question:** In MATLAB, how do you display the current working directory in the Command Window? **Answer:** Use the `pwd` command:

```matlab
pwd
```

2.3 Expressions and Variables

11. **Question:** Define a variable `x` with a value of 10 and a variable `y` with a value of 20. Then calculate and display their product in MATLAB. **Answer:**

```matlab
x = 10;
y = 20;
product = x * y;
disp(['The product is: ', num2str(product)]);
```

12. **Question:** Write a MATLAB expression to compute the square root of 16 and store the result in a variable `z`. **Answer:**

```matlab
z = sqrt(16);
```

13. **Question:** What will the following MATLAB code display?

```matlab
a = 10;
b = 20;
c = 5;
result = (a + b) * c;
disp(result);
```

Answer: The result will be:

150

14. **Question:** In MATLAB, how would you define a constant `PI` with the value `3.14159`?
    Answer:

```
PI = 3.14159;
```

15. **Question:** In MATLAB, write a program that performs the following:
    - o   Assign `100` to `a`
    - o   Assign `50` to `b`
    - o   Assign `a / b` to `c`
    - o   Display the value of `c`

    Answer:

```
a = 100;
b = 50;
c = a / b;
disp(['The value of c is: ', num2str(c)]);
```

CHAPTER 3: ARRAYS AND MATRICES IN MATLAB

3.1 Introduction to Arrays in MATLAB

Arrays are central to MATLAB programming, and the language is optimized for performing operations on arrays and matrices. This makes MATLAB particularly powerful for applications in linear algebra, scientific computing, and data analysis. Let's dive deeper into the concept of arrays, how to create and manipulate them, and how to use indexing and slicing to access elements in MATLAB.

Creating and Manipulating Arrays

Arrays in MATLAB can be one-dimensional (vectors) or multi-dimensional (matrices). Arrays are created using square brackets [], and you can populate them with numbers separated by spaces or commas for rows, and semicolons ; to indicate new rows.

One-Dimensional Arrays (Vectors)

A **vector** is a simple 1D array that contains a sequence of numbers, either in a single row (row vector) or in a single column (column vector).

- **Row Vector**: A row vector is a 1xN array (1 row and N columns).

```
% Creating a row vector
rowVec = [1, 2, 3, 4, 5];
```

- **Column Vector**: A column vector is an Nx1 array (N rows and 1 column).

```
% Creating a column vector
colVec = [1; 2; 3; 4; 5];
```

Two-Dimensional Arrays (Matrices)

A **matrix** is a 2D array, where data is arranged in rows and columns. You can create a matrix in MATLAB by separating elements in each row with spaces or commas, and separating rows with semicolons.

- **Matrix Example**: A 2x3 matrix with 2 rows and 3 columns.

```
% Creating a 2x3 matrix
matrix = [1, 2, 3; 4, 5, 6];
```

Manipulating Arrays

Once you've created arrays, you can manipulate them in various ways such as accessing specific elements, performing operations on them, or resizing them.

- **Element Access**: MATLAB uses **1-based indexing**, which means that the index of the first element is 1 (as opposed to C, which uses 0-based indexing). You can access a specific element of an array or matrix using parentheses ().

  For example, to access the element in the second row and third column of a matrix:

  ```
  % Accessing an element from a matrix
  element = matrix(2, 3);  % This accesses the element in the second row,
  third column (which is 6)
  ```

- **Resizing an Array**: In MATLAB, you can resize arrays dynamically. You can append new elements or rows and columns easily.

  For example, to add a new column to a matrix:

  ```
  % Resizing an array by appending a new column
  matrix = [matrix, [7; 8]];  % Adds a column [7; 8] to the existing
  matrix
  ```

- **Array Operations**: MATLAB supports a wide range of mathematical operations on arrays, including element-wise addition, multiplication, division, etc. You can perform **element-wise operations** using the . (dot) operator before arithmetic operators like +, *, /, and .^.

  For example, to add 1 to each element of a matrix, you would use:

  ```
  % Element-wise addition (adds 1 to each element of the matrix)
  result = matrix + 1;
  ```

  To perform element-wise multiplication, you would use the .* operator:

  ```
  % Element-wise multiplication (multiplies each element by 2)
  result = matrix .* 2;
  ```

Indexing and Slicing Arrays

In MATLAB, arrays can be accessed using **indexing** and **slicing**. Indexing refers to accessing specific elements or subarrays of an array, while slicing involves extracting a subarray or portion of an array.

Indexing Arrays

You can access individual elements, entire rows, or entire columns of an array using their indices. MATLAB uses **1-based indexing** to refer to array elements, which is important to note when accessing or modifying elements.

- **Accessing an Individual Element**: Use the indices in parentheses to access specific elements.

  For example, to get the second element of a row vector:

  ```
  % Accessing the second element of a row vector
  value = rowVec(2);   % This will return 2
  ```

- **Accessing an Entire Row or Column**:
  - To access an entire row of a matrix, you use the colon : to indicate all columns in that row. For example:

    ```
    % Accessing the entire second row
    row = matrix(2, :);   % This returns [4, 5, 6]
    ```

  - To access an entire column of a matrix, you use the colon : to indicate all rows in that column. For example:

    ```
    % Accessing the entire third column
    column = matrix(:, 3);   % This returns [3; 6]
    ```

Slicing Arrays

Slicing allows you to extract a subarray (i.e., a specific part) from a larger array or matrix. You can slice an array by specifying a range of indices.

- **Slicing a Matrix**: To extract a submatrix, specify the rows and columns you want to include using the start:end notation for both rows and columns.

  For example, to extract a submatrix that contains the first two rows and columns from the original matrix:

  ```
  % Extracting a sub-matrix from the top-left corner (first 2 rows and
  columns)
  subMatrix = matrix(1:2, 1:2);   % This extracts the first 2 rows and 2
  columns of the matrix
  ```

- **Extracting Specific Portions of a Row or Column**: You can also extract portions of a row or column using slicing.

  For example, to extract the second and third elements of the first row:

  ```
  % Extracting a specific portion of the first row (second to third
  elements)
  slice = matrix(1, 2:3);   % This returns [2, 3]
  ```

  Similarly, to extract the first two elements of the third column:

  ```
  % Extracting the first two elements of the third column
  ```

```
slice = matrix(1:2, 3);   % This returns [3; 6]
```

3.2 MATLAB vs C Arrays

Both **MATLAB** and **C** support arrays as fundamental data structures, but they differ significantly in terms of memory management, ease of use, and the way they handle multi-dimensional arrays and matrix operations. Let's explore these differences in detail.

Memory Management: MATLAB vs C

MATLAB Memory Management

MATLAB simplifies memory management, making it a powerful tool for numerical computations, especially when dealing with arrays and matrices.

1. **Automatic Memory Management**:
   MATLAB automatically manages memory allocation and deallocation. When you create arrays or perform operations on arrays, MATLAB takes care of the memory allocation without requiring explicit instructions from the programmer.
   - **Lazy Evaluation**:
     MATLAB employs a technique known as "lazy evaluation," which means it only performs calculations when necessary. For example, if you create a matrix and perform an operation on it, MATLAB will allocate the required memory dynamically when the operation is executed.
   - **Dynamic Array Size**:
     MATLAB arrays can grow or shrink as needed, and this is done automatically. You do not need to explicitly define the size of an array when you create it.

   Example:

   ```
   % MATLAB dynamically allocates memory when you run this
   A = rand(100, 100);   % Creates a 100x100 matrix of random numbers
   ```

   Here, MATLAB allocates memory for the `100x100` matrix at runtime. The size of `A` can also change dynamically based on further operations.

2. **Memory Efficiency**:
   MATLAB uses highly optimized data structures for storing arrays, allowing efficient memory utilization for large datasets and operations.

C Memory Management

In **C**, memory management is more manual and requires explicit instructions from the programmer. This provides flexibility but can also lead to errors if memory is not managed properly.

1. **Static Memory Allocation**:
   In C, you can define the size of an array at compile time. Once defined, the size of the array cannot change during runtime.

   Example:

   ```
   // Statically allocated array in C
   int arr[100];  // Fixed size, allocated at compile time
   ```

2. **Dynamic Memory Allocation**:
   C allows dynamic memory allocation using functions like `malloc` and `free`. These functions allocate and deallocate memory during runtime, giving you the flexibility to work with arrays whose size is not known in advance.

   Example:

   ```
   // Dynamically allocated array in C
   int *arr = (int*)malloc(100 * sizeof(int));  // Allocates memory for
   100 integers
   // Don't forget to free memory when done
   free(arr);
   ```

3. **Memory Deallocation**:
   Unlike MATLAB, where memory management is automatic, in C, you must explicitly deallocate memory using `free()` to prevent memory leaks. Forgetting to do this can lead to inefficient memory usage and crashes.

Multi-Dimensional Arrays and Matrix Operations

Multi-Dimensional Arrays in MATLAB

MATLAB is optimized for **multi-dimensional arrays**, including matrices and higher-dimensional arrays, making it an ideal environment for matrix-based operations. MATLAB natively supports multi-dimensional arrays, and it simplifies the manipulation of such arrays.

1. **Creating Multi-Dimensional Arrays**:
   You can easily create multi-dimensional arrays (such as 3D matrices) in MATLAB using functions like `reshape` or by directly specifying the dimensions.

   Example:

   ```
   % Creating a 3D array (2x2x2 matrix)
   ```

```
A = reshape(1:8, [2, 2, 2]);  % Reshapes a vector into a 2x2x2 3D
matrix
```

2. Matrix Operations:

MATLAB is designed to perform matrix operations efficiently. You can directly use operators to perform matrix multiplication, element-wise operations, and transpose operations.

- **Matrix Multiplication**:

```
% Matrix multiplication (inner product of matrices)
result = A * B;
```

- **Element-wise Operations**: To perform operations on corresponding elements of two matrices (or arrays), MATLAB uses the .* operator for element-wise multiplication, ./ for element-wise division, etc.

```
% Element-wise multiplication (multiplies corresponding elements)
result = A .* B;
```

- **Transpose**: The transpose of a matrix is easily computed using the apostrophe (').

```
% Transpose of a matrix
result = A';  % A' returns the transpose of matrix A
```

MATLAB vs C for Matrix Operations

In **C**, performing matrix operations like multiplication requires writing explicit code to loop through the rows and columns of matrices. This manual approach gives you full control over the operations but also requires more effort and potential for errors.

1. Manual Matrix Operations in C:

In C, if you want to multiply two matrices, you need to loop over the rows and columns, manually computing the dot product of the rows and columns.

Example (Matrix Multiplication in C):

```
// Example of manual matrix multiplication in C
int A[2][2] = {{1, 2}, {3, 4}};
int B[2][2] = {{5, 6}, {7, 8}};
int result[2][2];

// Matrix multiplication
for (int i = 0; i < 2; i++) {
    for (int j = 0; j < 2; j++) {
        result[i][j] = 0;
        for (int k = 0; k < 2; k++) {
            result[i][j] += A[i][k] * B[k][j];
        }
    }
}
```

```
}
```

In this example, three nested `for` loops are needed to compute the matrix product. The code can quickly become complex and error-prone as the matrices grow larger.

2. **Matrix Operations in MATLAB**:
MATLAB significantly simplifies matrix operations. Matrix multiplication, element-wise operations, and transposition can be performed with just a single line of code. This simplicity is one of MATLAB's key strengths.

Example (Matrix Multiplication in MATLAB):

```
A = [1, 2; 3, 4];
B = [5, 6; 7, 8];
result = A * B;  % Matrix multiplication (inner product of A and B)
```

In this example, matrix multiplication is performed with a single line of code, and MATLAB handles the internal looping and memory management for you.

Summary of Differences: MATLAB vs C Arrays

Aspect	MATLAB	C
Memory Management	Automatic memory management (dynamic allocation)	Manual memory management (static or dynamic)
Array Size	Dynamically resizable during runtime	Fixed size (static) or manually managed (dynamic)
Multi-Dimensional Arrays	Easy to work with multi-dimensional arrays	Requires manual indexing and loops for multi-dimensional arrays
Matrix Operations	Built-in support for matrix operations	Requires explicit looping and manual handling of operations
Ease of Use	Simple, one-line operations for matrices	Complex, multiple lines of code for matrix operations

25 multiple-choice questions (MCQs)

3.1 Introduction to Arrays in MATLAB

Creating and Manipulating Arrays

1. **Which of the following creates a row vector in MATLAB?**
    a) `rowVec = [1; 2; 3]`

b) `rowVec = [1, 2, 3]`
c) `rowVec = (1, 2, 3)`
d) `rowVec = {1, 2, 3}`

Answer: b) `rowVec = [1, 2, 3]`

2. **How do you create a 2x3 matrix in MATLAB?**
   a) `matrix = [1, 2, 3; 4, 5, 6]`
   b) `matrix = [1, 2, 3, 4, 5, 6]`
   c) `matrix = (1 2 3, 4 5 6)`
   d) `matrix = {1, 2, 3, 4, 5, 6}`

   Answer: a) `matrix = [1, 2, 3; 4, 5, 6]`

3. **What is the result of the following code?**
   `A = [1, 2, 3]; A = A + 1;`
   a) `[1, 2, 3]`
   b) `[2, 3, 4]`
   c) `2`
   d) `None of the above`

   Answer: b) `[2, 3, 4]`

4. **Which operator is used for element-wise multiplication in MATLAB?**
   a) `*`
   b) `.`
   c) `.*`
   d) `//`

   Answer: c) `.*`

5. **How do you access the element at the 2nd row, 3rd column in a matrix A?**
   a) `A(2, 3)`
   b) `A(3, 2)`
   c) `A[2, 3]`
   d) `A{2, 3}`

   Answer: a) `A(2, 3)`

6. **What does the following code do in MATLAB?**
   `A = [1, 2, 3; 4, 5, 6]; B = A + 10;`
   a) Adds 10 to each element of matrix A
   b) Adds 10 to each row of matrix A
   c) Adds 10 to each column of matrix A
   d) None of the above

Answer: a) Adds 10 to each element of matrix A

7. **Which of the following is the correct syntax for creating a column vector in MATLAB?**
   a) `colVec = [1; 2; 3]`
   b) `colVec = (1, 2, 3)`
   c) `colVec = [1 2 3]`
   d) `colVec = {1, 2, 3}`

   Answer: a) `colVec = [1; 2; 3]`

8. **How do you extract the first two rows and columns from a matrix A?**
   a) `A(1:2, 1:2)`
   b) `A(2:1, 2:1)`
   c) `A{1:2, 1:2}`
   d) `A[1:2, 1:2]`

   Answer: a) `A(1:2, 1:2)`

9. **What does the colon operator (`:`) do when used in array indexing?**
   a) It specifies all elements of a row or column
   b) It specifies the element at the end of a row or column
   c) It transposes the matrix
   d) It multiplies each element of the array

   Answer: a) It specifies all elements of a row or column

10. **What is the result of `A = [1, 2, 3; 4, 5, 6]; B = A(:, 2);`?**
    a) The second column of matrix A
    b) The second row of matrix A
    c) The element at index 2 of matrix A
    d) A matrix with two columns

    Answer: a) The second column of matrix A

Indexing and Slicing Arrays

11. **What will `matrix(1, 2:3)` return in MATLAB?**
    a) The first row of the matrix
    b) The second and third columns of the first row
    c) The second and third rows of the first column
    d) An error

    Answer: b) The second and third columns of the first row

12. **Which of the following is true about MATLAB's array indexing?**
    a) MATLAB uses 0-based indexing
    b) MATLAB uses 1-based indexing
    c) MATLAB uses both 0-based and 1-based indexing
    d) MATLAB does not support array indexing

    Answer: b) MATLAB uses 1-based indexing

13. **What does the following command do in MATLAB?**
    `A = [1, 2, 3]; A = A .* 2;`
    a) Doubles the entire array
    b) Doubles each element in the array
    c) Adds 2 to each element
    d) None of the above

    Answer: b) Doubles each element in the array

14. **Which of the following will resize an array in MATLAB?**
    a) `resize(A)`
    b) `A = [A, [7; 8]]`
    c) `reshape(A)`
    d) `expand(A)`

    Answer: b) `A = [A, [7; 8]]`

3.2 MATLAB vs C Arrays

Memory Management: MATLAB vs C

15. **Which of the following is true about memory management in MATLAB?**
    a) Memory management in MATLAB is done manually by the programmer
    b) MATLAB handles memory allocation automatically
    c) MATLAB does not support dynamic memory allocation
    d) MATLAB requires the use of `malloc` for memory allocation

    Answer: b) MATLAB handles memory allocation automatically

16. **In C, how do you allocate memory for a dynamic array?**
    a) `int arr[100];`
    b) `int* arr = malloc(100 * sizeof(int));`
    c) `int arr = dynamic(100);`
    d) `int* arr = new int[100];`

    Answer: b) `int* arr = malloc(100 * sizeof(int));`

17. **What is the key difference in memory management between MATLAB and C?**
    a) MATLAB uses `malloc` for dynamic memory allocation
    b) C handles memory automatically, unlike MATLAB
    c) MATLAB automatically manages memory while C requires manual memory management
    d) C has built-in support for dynamic arrays, unlike MATLAB

    Answer: c) MATLAB automatically manages memory while C requires manual memory management

18. **Which of the following functions is used to deallocate memory in C?**
    a) `free()`
    b) `delete()`
    c) `clear()`
    d) `remove()`

    Answer: a) `free()`

19. **How does MATLAB handle memory resizing for arrays?**
    a) Memory must be manually resized using `resize()`
    b) Memory resizing is automatic and transparent to the user
    c) You must use a special function for resizing arrays
    d) Arrays cannot be resized in MATLAB

    Answer: b) Memory resizing is automatic and transparent to the user

---

Multi-Dimensional Arrays and Matrix Operations

20. **How do you create a 3D array in MATLAB?**
    a) `A = reshape(1:8, [2, 2, 2]);`
    b) `A = 2D array;`
    c) `A = [1 2 3; 4 5 6]`
    d) `A = {1, 2, 3, 4, 5, 6}`

    Answer: a) `A = reshape(1:8, [2, 2, 2]);`

21. **What does `A * B` do in MATLAB when `A` and `B` are matrices?**
    a) Performs element-wise multiplication
    b) Adds the two matrices
    c) Performs matrix multiplication (inner product)
    d) Multiplies all the elements of `A` and `B`

    Answer: c) Performs matrix multiplication (inner product)

22. **In MATLAB, which operator is used for element-wise division?**
    a) /
    b) //
    c) ./
    d) *

    Answer: c) ./

23. **How would you transpose a matrix in MATLAB?**
    a) `transpose(A)`
    b) `A.'`
    c) `A.T()`
    d) `A_flip()`

    Answer: b) `A.'`

24. **In C, how do you perform matrix multiplication?**
    a) Using the * operator
    b) Using a loop to manually calculate the dot product
    c) Using the `multiply()` function
    d) Using the `matrix_multiply()` function

    Answer: b) Using a loop to manually calculate the dot product

25. **Which of the following statements is true regarding matrix operations in MATLAB?**
    a) MATLAB requires you to manually loop through matrices to perform operations
    b) Matrix multiplication is a single line of code in MATLAB
    c) MATLAB does not support matrix operations
    d) MATLAB uses `malloc` to handle matrix operations

    Answer: b) Matrix multiplication is a single line of code in MATLAB

3.1 Introduction to Arrays in MATLAB

Creating and Manipulating Arrays

1. **Question**: Write a MATLAB script to create a row vector v with values from 1 to 5.
   Then, add 3 to each element of the vector.

   Answer:

```
v = [1, 2, 3, 4, 5];
v = v + 3;
disp(v);   % Output: [4, 5, 6, 7, 8]
```

2. **Question**: Create a 3x3 matrix in MATLAB with values from 1 to 9. Perform element-wise multiplication by 2.

   Answer:

   ```
   A = [1, 2, 3; 4, 5, 6; 7, 8, 9];
   A = A .* 2;
   disp(A);  % Output: [2, 4, 6; 8, 10, 12; 14, 16, 18]
   ```

3. **Question**: Create a column vector v with values [5; 10; 15; 20] and then find the sum of all elements in the vector.

   Answer:

   ```
   v = [5; 10; 15; 20];
   total = sum(v);
   disp(total);  % Output: 50
   ```

4. **Question**: Create a 2x3 matrix A and resize it to a 3x2 matrix. Show both the original and resized matrices.

   Answer:

   ```
   A = [1, 2, 3; 4, 5, 6];
   disp(A);  % Output: [1, 2, 3; 4, 5, 6]
   A = reshape(A, 3, 2);
   disp(A);  % Output: [1, 2; 3, 4; 5, 6]
   ```

5. **Question**: Create a 3x3 matrix B and find the element in the second row and third column.

   Answer:

   ```
   B = [1, 2, 3; 4, 5, 6; 7, 8, 9];
   element = B(2, 3);
   disp(element);  % Output: 6
   ```

Indexing and Slicing Arrays

6. **Question**: Create a 4x4 matrix M and extract the first row and second column.

   Answer:

   ```
   M = [1, 2, 3, 4; 5, 6, 7, 8; 9, 10, 11, 12; 13, 14, 15, 16];
   row = M(1, :);  % Extract first row
   column = M(:, 2);  % Extract second column
   disp(row);  % Output: [1, 2, 3, 4]
   disp(column);  % Output: [2; 6; 10; 14]
   ```

7. **Question**: Extract a submatrix from `M` (from row 2 to row 3, and column 2 to column 3).

Answer:

```
subMatrix = M(2:3, 2:3);
disp(subMatrix);   % Output: [6, 7; 10, 11]
```

8. **Question**: Given the vector `v = [10, 20, 30, 40, 50]`, extract the second and fourth elements.

Answer:

```
v = [10, 20, 30, 40, 50];
elements = v([2, 4]);
disp(elements);   % Output: [20, 40]
```

9. **Question**: Using the vector `v = [1, 2, 3, 4, 5]`, extract a slice that includes the second to the fourth elements.

Answer:

```
v = [1, 2, 3, 4, 5];
slice = v(2:4);
disp(slice);   % Output: [2, 3, 4]
```

10. **Question**: Create a 2x2 matrix and transpose it. Show both the original and transposed matrices.

Answer:

```
A = [1, 2; 3, 4];
disp(A);   % Output: [1, 2; 3, 4]
A_transposed = A';
disp(A_transposed);   % Output: [1, 3; 2, 4]
```

3.2 MATLAB vs C Arrays

Memory Management: MATLAB vs C

11. **Question**: In C, allocate memory for an array of 10 integers using `malloc`. Write the code and free the memory after use.

Answer:

```
int* arr = (int*)malloc(10 * sizeof(int));   // Allocate memory
// Use the array...
free(arr);   // Free the allocated memory
```

12. **Question**: In MATLAB, create a 5x5 matrix and explain how MATLAB automatically handles memory allocation when you create this matrix.

Answer:

```
M = rand(5, 5);   % Create a 5x5 matrix with random values
% MATLAB automatically allocates memory for the matrix behind the scenes
disp(M);
```

13. **Question**: In C, if you want to dynamically allocate memory for an array and ensure it is freed when no longer needed, what function do you use?

Answer:

```
free(arr);   // Used to free dynamically allocated memory in C
```

14. **Question**: Explain the difference between static and dynamic memory allocation for arrays in C. Provide a code example for dynamic memory allocation.

Answer: Static allocation allocates memory at compile time and the size is fixed, while dynamic allocation allocates memory during runtime using functions like `malloc`.

```
// Static allocation:
int arr[10];   // Fixed size at compile time

// Dynamic allocation:
int* arr = (int*)malloc(10 * sizeof(int));   // Size determined at runtime
```

15. **Question**: Compare the handling of memory for arrays in MATLAB and C. Why is memory management easier in MATLAB?

Answer:

- In MATLAB, memory management is automatic. You don't need to manually allocate or deallocate memory. The arrays grow dynamically as needed.
- In C, memory must be allocated and deallocated manually using functions like `malloc` and `free`. This makes memory management more complex and prone to errors like memory leaks.

Multi-Dimensional Arrays and Matrix Operations

16. **Question**: In MATLAB, create a 2x3 matrix and perform matrix multiplication with another compatible matrix.

Answer:

```
A = [1, 2, 3; 4, 5, 6];
B = [7, 8; 9, 10; 11, 12];
result = A * B;  % Matrix multiplication
disp(result);  % Output: [58, 64; 139, 154]
```

17. **Question**: In MATLAB, create a 3D array of dimensions 2x2x2 and perform element-wise addition with another 3D array of the same size.

Answer:

```
A = reshape(1:8, [2, 2, 2]);
B = reshape(8:-1:1, [2, 2, 2]);
result = A + B;  % Element-wise addition
disp(result);  % Output:  [9, 11; 13, 15] and [15, 13; 11, 9]
```

18. **Question**: In MATLAB, if you have a matrix A with dimensions 3x3, how would you transpose the matrix?

Answer:

```
A = [1, 2, 3; 4, 5, 6; 7, 8, 9];
A_transposed = A';
disp(A_transposed);  % Output: [1, 4, 7; 2, 5, 8; 3, 6, 9]
```

19. **Question**: Write C code to perform matrix multiplication for two 2x2 matrices A and B manually.

Answer:

```
int A[2][2] = {{1, 2}, {3, 4}};
int B[2][2] = {{5, 6}, {7, 8}};
int result[2][2] = {{0, 0}, {0, 0}};
for (int i = 0; i < 2; i++) {
    for (int j = 0; j < 2; j++) {
        for (int k = 0; k < 2; k++) {
            result[i][j] += A[i][k] * B[k][j];
        }
    }
}
// Display result matrix
```

20. **Question**: How would you perform element-wise multiplication of two matrices A and B in MATLAB?

Answer:

```
A = [1, 2, 3; 4, 5, 6];
B = [1, 1, 1; 2, 2, 2];
result = A .* B;  % Element-wise multiplication
disp(result);  % Output: [1, 2, 3; 8, 10, 12]
```

21. **Question**: What is the result of multiplying a 3x3 matrix by a scalar in MATLAB?

Answer:

```
A = [1, 2, 3; 4, 5, 6; 7, 8, 9];
result = A * 2;  % Matrix by scalar multiplication
disp(result);  % Output: [2, 4, 6; 8, 10, 12; 14, 16, 18]
```

CHAPTER 4: PLOTTING AND VISUALIZATION

4.1 Basic Plotting in MATLAB

MATLAB is a powerful tool for visualizing data, and its plotting capabilities make it a go-to choice for data analysis, scientific computing, and engineering applications. It has several built-in functions for creating plots that make it easy to visualize data in various ways. This section covers the basics of plotting in MATLAB, including **line plots**, **bar plots**, **scatter plots**, and how to **customize plots** using labels, titles, and legends.

Line Plots

Line plots are one of the most commonly used ways to visualize data. They display data points connected by straight lines, which is helpful for observing trends, patterns, or relationships in the data.

Creating a Line Plot

To create a line plot, you need two vectors: one for the x-values and one for the y-values. The plot function is used to create line plots in MATLAB.

Example:

```
x = 0:0.1:10;    % x values from 0 to 10, with an increment of 0.1
y = sin(x);      % y values as the sine of x

plot(x, y);      % Create a line plot
```

In this example:

- x = 0:0.1:10; generates a vector from 0 to 10 with increments of 0.1.
- y = sin(x); calculates the sine of each value in x.
- plot(x, y); generates a plot where x is on the x-axis and y is on the y-axis. By default, MATLAB connects these data points with straight lines.

Bar Plots

Bar plots are useful for visualizing categorical data or comparing values across different categories. They display data using rectangular bars, where the height of each bar represents the value of the data.

Creating a Bar Plot

The `bar` function is used to create bar plots in MATLAB.

Example:

```
x = [1, 2, 3, 4, 5];        % Categories on the x-axis
y = [10, 20, 30, 40, 50];   % Corresponding values

bar(x, y);   % Create a bar plot
```

In this example:

- `x = [1, 2, 3, 4, 5];` specifies the categories for the x-axis.
- `y = [10, 20, 30, 40, 50];` specifies the heights of the bars.
- `bar(x, y);` generates a vertical bar plot where each bar's height is determined by the corresponding value in `y`.

The bars in this plot represent the data visually, and the x-axis corresponds to the categories, while the y-axis corresponds to the values.

Scatter Plots

Scatter plots are useful for displaying individual data points and visualizing relationships between two variables. Each point in the plot represents a pair of values, one from the x-axis and one from the y-axis.

Creating a Scatter Plot

The `scatter` function is used to create scatter plots in MATLAB.

Example:

```
x = rand(1, 50);    % 50 random x values between 0 and 1
y = rand(1, 50);    % 50 random y values between 0 and 1

scatter(x, y);      % Create a scatter plot
```

In this example:

- `x = rand(1, 50);` generates 50 random values for the x-axis.
- `y = rand(1, 50);` generates 50 random values for the y-axis.
- `scatter(x, y);` generates a scatter plot where each point's position is determined by the corresponding x and y values.

Scatter plots are often used to identify trends, clusters, or correlations between variables.

Customizing Plots: Labels, Legends, and Titles

Once you have created your plot, you will often need to enhance it by adding **labels**, **titles**, and **legends** to make it more informative and easier to interpret.

Adding Labels

Adding labels to the x-axis and y-axis helps explain what each axis represents.

1. **x-axis Label:** The `xlabel` function is used to add a label to the x-axis.

   ```
   xlabel('Time (seconds)');  % Label for x-axis
   ```

2. **y-axis Label:** The `ylabel` function is used to add a label to the y-axis.

   ```
   ylabel('Amplitude');       % Label for y-axis
   ```

Example:

```
x = 0:0.1:10;            % x values from 0 to 10
y = sin(x);              % y values as the sine of x
plot(x, y);              % Create a line plot
xlabel('Time (seconds)');  % Label for x-axis
ylabel('Amplitude');       % Label for y-axis
```

In this example:

- `xlabel('Time (seconds)');` adds a label to the x-axis indicating the time.
- `ylabel('Amplitude');` adds a label to the y-axis indicating the amplitude of the sine wave.

Adding a Title

Titles are important for providing context to the plot. The `title` function is used to add a title to the plot.

Example:

```
title('Sine Wave');  % Add a title to the plot
```

Example with Complete Plot:

```
x = 0:0.1:10;            % x values from 0 to 10
y = sin(x);              % y values as the sine of x
```

```
plot(x, y);              % Create a line plot
xlabel('Time (seconds)');
ylabel('Amplitude');
title('Sine Wave');      % Add a title to the plot
```

The `title` function adds the text "Sine Wave" at the top of the plot.

Adding a Legend

When you have multiple data series in a single plot, it's useful to include a **legend** to distinguish between them. The `legend` function is used to create a legend that maps the data series to labels.

Example:

```
x = 0:0.1:10;            % x values from 0 to 10
y1 = sin(x);             % First data series (sine)
y2 = cos(x);             % Second data series (cosine)

plot(x, y1, 'r');        % Plot sine wave in red
hold on;
plot(x, y2, 'b');        % Plot cosine wave in blue
legend('sin(x)', 'cos(x)');  % Add a legend
```

In this example:

- `plot(x, y1, 'r');` plots the sine wave in red.
- `plot(x, y2, 'b');` plots the cosine wave in blue.
- `legend('sin(x)', 'cos(x)');` creates a legend that labels the two curves.

The `hold on` command is used to add multiple plots to the same figure without overwriting the previous plot.

4.2 Built-in Functions for Data Visualization

MATLAB has a rich set of built-in functions for visualizing data. These functions simplify the process of creating various types of plots and charts, and they come with numerous options for customizing the appearance.

Using Built-in MATLAB Functions for Plotting

MATLAB includes a number of built-in functions for creating specialized plots such as histograms, pie charts, and more. Examples include:

1. **Histogram Plot:**

```matlab
data = randn(1, 1000);   % Generate random data
histogram(data);         % Plot histogram
```

2. **Pie Chart:**

```matlab
data = [10, 20, 30, 40];
pie(data);                    % Plot pie chart
```

3. **Surface Plot:** Surface plots are used to display 3D data.

```matlab
[X, Y] = meshgrid(-5:0.1:5, -5:0.1:5);
Z = X.^2 + Y.^2;
surf(X, Y, Z);               % Create a surface plot
```

Comparing Plotting Techniques in C and MATLAB

In C, plotting requires additional libraries and manual handling, whereas MATLAB is purpose-built for plotting, making it much simpler to create and customize graphs. Below is a comparison:

- **C**: You need to manually manage data structures (arrays), and plotting typically requires external libraries such as `gnuplot` or custom code to output data to a file.
- **MATLAB**: Built-in functions make it easier to create plots with minimal code. MATLAB automatically handles data structures and plot rendering.

In MATLAB, plotting is done with a single function call, such as `plot(x, y)`, whereas in C, you would need to write additional code to visualize the data or use a library for plotting.

4.3 Generating Waveforms and Sound Replay

MATLAB is not just a tool for numerical computations and data analysis, but also a powerful environment for generating and manipulating sound signals. It can generate different types of waveforms, such as **sine**, **square**, and **triangle waves**, which are fundamental in audio processing, signal analysis, and sound synthesis. Additionally, MATLAB allows you to play sound files and generated waveforms, making it ideal for sound experimentation and audio applications.

Sine, Square, and Triangle Waves

These are basic types of waveforms commonly used in signal processing, audio synthesis, and various other applications. Let's break down how to generate and plot these waveforms in MATLAB.

---

1. Sine Wave

A **sine wave** is a smooth periodic oscillation that represents the simplest form of a sound wave. It is often used in audio synthesis and testing. The sine wave equation is:

$y(t)=\sin(2\pi ft)$ $y(t) = \sin(2\pi f t)$ $y(t)=\sin(2\pi ft)$

Where:

- f is the frequency of the wave (how many oscillations per second).
- t is the time vector.

Generating and Plotting a Sine Wave in MATLAB

```
t = 0:0.01:1;          % Time vector from 0 to 1 second with a 0.01-second
step
f = 5;                 % Frequency of the sine wave (5 Hz)
y = sin(2*pi*f*t);     % Generate the sine wave for the given time vector
and frequency
plot(t, y);            % Plot the sine wave
```

In this example:

- The `t` vector defines the time range from 0 to 1 second with an increment of 0.01 seconds.
- `f = 5` defines the frequency of the sine wave (5 cycles per second).
- `y = sin(2*pi*f*t)` generates the sine wave.
- `plot(t, y)` plots the sine wave against time.

---

2. Square Wave

A **square wave** is a non-sinusoidal waveform that alternates between two levels, typically high (1) and low (0), with a defined frequency. It's often used in digital systems and audio synthesis.

Generating and Plotting a Square Wave in MATLAB

```
y = square(2*pi*f*t);   % Generate a square wave with the same frequency f
plot(t, y);             % Plot the square wave
```

In this example:

- `square(2*pi*f*t)` generates a square wave at a frequency of fff Hz.
- The `plot(t, y)` function is used to plot the square wave over time.

3. Triangle Wave

A **triangle wave** is a waveform that oscillates linearly between a maximum and minimum value, resembling a series of triangles. It's often used in audio signal synthesis and testing.

Generating and Plotting a Triangle Wave in MATLAB

```
y = sawtooth(2*pi*f*t, 0.5);   % Generate a triangle wave (0.5 is the duty
cycle)
plot(t, y);                    % Plot the triangle wave
```

In this example:

- `sawtooth(2*pi*f*t, 0.5)` generates a triangle wave. The second parameter `0.5` specifies that the waveform should have a 50% duty cycle, meaning the high and low times of the waveform are equal.
- `plot(t, y)` is used to visualize the triangle wave.

Playing Sound Files in MATLAB

MATLAB also allows you to work with audio data, load sound files, and play them. This feature is helpful when working with audio signals, sound generation, or audio analysis.

1. Playing a Sound

To play an audio file in MATLAB, you first need to read the sound file using the `audioread` function, and then you can play it using the `sound` function.

Example: Playing a Sound File

```
[y, Fs] = audioread('soundfile.wav');   % Read the audio file into 'y' and
sample rate 'Fs'
sound(y, Fs);                           % Play the sound using the sample rate
'Fs'
```

In this example:

- `audioread('soundfile.wav')` loads the audio file `'soundfile.wav'`. The audio data is stored in the variable `y`, and the sample rate is stored in `Fs`.
- `sound(y, Fs)` plays the sound stored in `y` at the sample rate `Fs`.

2. Playing a Generated Waveform

You can also generate waveforms programmatically and play them back. For example, after generating a sine wave, you can use the `sound` function to play it as audio.

Example: Playing a Sine Wave Sound

```
t = 0:0.01:1;          % Time vector from 0 to 1 second
f = 5;                 % Frequency of the sine wave (5 Hz)
y = sin(2*pi*f*t);     % Generate the sine wave
Fs = 1000;             % Sampling frequency (samples per second)

sound(y, Fs);          % Play the sine wave sound at the given sampling rate
```

In this example:

- The sine wave is generated with a frequency of 5 Hz.
- `Fs = 1000` specifies the sampling rate of the audio signal (1000 samples per second).
- `sound(y, Fs)` plays the sine wave using the `sound` function.

4.4 Saving and Loading Data

MATLAB provides simple and efficient methods for saving and loading data, which is essential for managing large datasets, storing results, or working with data across multiple sessions. These capabilities support the process of persisting data to disk, retrieving it, and sharing it between different programs or sessions. MATLAB includes both high-level functions for saving/loading data and lower-level file I/O functions for more custom or formatted data handling.

File I/O in MATLAB: `save`, `load`, and `fopen`

MATLAB provides several built-in functions to handle file input and output (I/O). Below are the key functions you'll use for saving and loading data, along with examples of how they work.

1. Saving Data

In MATLAB, you can save variables or matrices to a file using the `save` function. The most common format used for saving data is the `.mat` file format, which is MATLAB's native format for storing variables. You can save entire workspaces or specific variables to these files.

Example: Saving Data to a `.mat` File

```
A = rand(10, 10);           % Create a 10x10 matrix with random values
save('datafile.mat', 'A');  % Save the matrix 'A' to a file named
'datafile.mat'
```

In this example:

- The variable `A` is created as a 10x10 matrix containing random values.
- The `save` function stores the matrix `A` in a file called `datafile.mat`. The `.mat` extension is the default format for storing MATLAB variables.
- You can also save multiple variables at once by separating them with commas, for example: `save('datafile.mat', 'A', 'B', 'C');`

---

2. Loading Data

To load previously saved data from a `.mat` file into your MATLAB workspace, use the `load` function. This loads all variables saved in the file or specific variables by name.

Example: Loading Data from a `.mat` File

```
load('datafile.mat');    % Load all variables from the file 'datafile.mat'
disp(A);                 % Display the matrix A that was loaded
```

In this example:

- The `load('datafile.mat')` command loads the saved variable(s) from the file into the current workspace.
- `disp(A)` displays the matrix `A` which was loaded from the file.

You can also load specific variables from a file by specifying their names, like so:

```
load('datafile.mat', 'A');  % Load only the variable 'A' from the file
```

---

4. **Writing to a Text File**
   In addition to the `.mat` format, you can write data to text files using MATLAB's `fopen`, `fprintf`, and `fclose` functions. This allows you to store data in a human-readable format (e.g., CSV, plain text).

Example: Writing Data to a Text File

```
fileID = fopen('output.txt', 'w');  % Open file 'output.txt' for writing ('w' mode)
fprintf(fileID, '%f %f\n', A);       % Write the matrix 'A' to the text file
fclose(fileID);                      % Close the file
```

In this example:

- `fopen('output.txt', 'w')` opens the file `output.txt` in write mode. If the file doesn't exist, MATLAB will create it.
- `fprintf(fileID, '%f %f\n', A)` writes the contents of `A` to the file. The format specifier `%f` is used for writing floating-point numbers, and the newline character `\n` is used to separate rows of data.
- `fclose(fileID)` closes the file after writing is complete.

You can use similar functions like `fread`, `fwrite`, or `fgetl` to read and write more complex data types or binary data, but `fprintf` and `fopen` are commonly used for simple text-based file operations.

MATLAB vs C File Handling

MATLAB simplifies file I/O by providing high-level functions such as `save`, `load`, `fopen`, `fprintf`, and `fclose`. These functions abstract away much of the complexity involved in file handling. In contrast, **C** requires more detailed manual management of files, such as dealing with **file pointers**, ensuring proper formats for binary or text files, and performing operations on raw byte data.

MATLAB File Handling Advantages:

1. **Simplicity**: Functions like `save` and `load` make it easy to read and write variables without needing to worry about file pointers or formats.
2. **MATLAB-Specific Formats**: The `.mat` file format is MATLAB's native data storage format, making it easier to store and retrieve variables in their original types (e.g., matrices, arrays).
3. **Efficient Data Management**: MATLAB handles memory and storage efficiently, so you don't need to worry about low-level memory management.

C File Handling:

C requires you to manually handle file opening, reading, writing, and closing. The following is an example of how you might write to a text file in **C**:

Example: Writing Data to a Text File in C

```c
#include <stdio.h>

int main() {
    FILE *file = fopen("data.txt", "w");  // Open file for writing ('w' mode)
    if (file == NULL) {  // Check for successful file opening
        printf("Error opening file.\n");
        return 1;
    }
    fprintf(file, "Data: %d\n", 100);  // Write an integer to the file
    fclose(file);  // Close the file
    return 0;
}
```

In this C example:

- `fopen("data.txt", "w")` opens the file `data.txt` for writing.
- `fprintf(file, "Data: %d\n", 100)` writes the data (integer 100) to the file.
- `fclose(file)` closes the file after writing.

C File Handling Challenges:

- **Manual Memory Management**: In C, you need to manage file pointers (like `FILE *file`), check for successful file opening, and ensure that data is properly written in the correct format.
- **Error Handling**: C requires explicit error checks (e.g., checking if `fopen` succeeded).
- **File Formats**: You must decide whether you want to work with plain text or binary data and then handle the reading/writing operations accordingly.

25 multiple-choice questions (MCQs)

4.1 Basic Plotting in MATLAB

1. Which of the following functions is used to create a line plot in MATLAB?
A) `bar`
B) `plot`
C) `scatter`
D) `histogram`
Answer: B) `plot`

2. Which of the following generates a bar plot in MATLAB?
A) `plot`
B) `scatter`
C) `bar`

D) `stem`
Answer: C) `bar`

3. How do you generate a scatter plot in MATLAB?
A) `plot(x, y)`
B) `bar(x, y)`
C) `scatter(x, y)`
D) `line(x, y)`
Answer: C) `scatter(x, y)`

4. What is the default behavior of the `plot` function in MATLAB?
A) It displays a bar chart.
B) It connects data points with lines.
C) It displays a scatter plot.
D) It creates a 3D surface plot.
Answer: B) It connects data points with lines.

5. How would you add a title to a plot in MATLAB?
A) `title('Your Title')`
B) `xlabel('Your Title')`
C) `legend('Your Title')`
D) `ylabel('Your Title')`
Answer: A) `title('Your Title')`

6. Which function is used to label the x-axis in MATLAB?
A) `title`
B) `legend`
C) `xlabel`
D) `ylabel`
Answer: C) `xlabel`

7. How can you add a legend to a MATLAB plot?
A) `addlegend('Label1')`
B) `legend('Label1')`
C) `addTitle('Title')`
D) `title('Label1')`
Answer: B) `legend('Label1')`

8. What does the `hold on` command do in MATLAB?
A) It stops adding new data to the plot.
B) It allows multiple plots to be overlaid on the same figure.
C) It generates a grid for the plot.
D) It removes the previous plot.
Answer: B) It allows multiple plots to be overlaid on the same figure.

9. Which function in MATLAB is used to specify the limits of the axes?

A) `setAxesLimits()`
B) `xlim()` and `ylim()`
C) `axisLimits()`
D) `limits()`
Answer: B) `xlim()` and `ylim()`

10. In the plot command `plot(x, y, 'r')`, what does the `'r'` signify?
A) Red color for the plot.
B) Solid line.
C) Circle markers.
D) Yellow color for the plot.
Answer: A) Red color for the plot.

4.2 Built-in Functions for Data Visualization

11. Which MATLAB function can be used to plot a sine wave?
A) `plot`
B) `sin`
C) `scatter`
D) `wave`
Answer: A) `plot` (using `sin` for the data)

12. Which of the following is the MATLAB function to display a histogram?
A) `hist`
B) `scatter`
C) `bar`
D) `histogram`
Answer: D) `histogram`

13. What is the default behavior of the `plot3` function in MATLAB?
A) It plots data points in 2D.
B) It plots data points in 3D.
C) It generates a contour plot.
D) It plots a pie chart.
Answer: B) It plots data points in 3D.

14. Which MATLAB function is used to plot data as a surface?
A) `scatter`
B) `surf`
C) `bar`
D) `mesh`
Answer: B) `surf`

15. MATLAB provides which built-in function to add grid lines to a plot?
A) `grid on`
B) `addGrid()`
C) `addLines()`
D) `showGrid()`
Answer: A) `grid on`

16. How can you compare plotting techniques in MATLAB and C?
A) MATLAB requires manual loops for plotting, while C does not.
B) MATLAB has built-in high-level functions for plotting, while C requires manually handling arrays and plotting.
C) Both MATLAB and C use the same plotting functions.
D) C has built-in functions for plotting, while MATLAB requires manual calculations.
Answer: B) MATLAB has built-in high-level functions for plotting, while C requires manually handling arrays and plotting.

4.3 Generating Waveforms and Sound Replay

17. How can you generate a sine wave in MATLAB?
A) `y = sin(2 * pi * f * t)`
B) `y = square(t)`
C) `y = sin(t)`
D) `y = tri(t)`
Answer: A) `y = sin(2 * pi * f * t)`

18. Which MATLAB function generates a square wave?
A) `square`
B) `sin`
C) `sawtooth`
D) `triangle`
Answer: A) `square`

19. How would you generate a triangle wave in MATLAB?
A) `y = triangle(t)`
B) `y = sawtooth(t)`
C) `y = square(t)`
D) `y = sawtooth(t, 0.5)`
Answer: D) `y = sawtooth(t, 0.5)`

20. What is the purpose of the `sound` function in MATLAB?
A) To generate waveforms.
B) To play sound from an audio file.
C) To plot data.

D) To stop playing sound.
Answer: B) To play sound from an audio file.

21. How do you play a generated waveform in MATLAB?
A) `playSound(waveform)`
B) `sound(waveform)`
C) `replaySound(waveform)`
D) `play(waveform)`
Answer: B) `sound(waveform)`

4.4 Saving and Loading Data

22. What function is used in MATLAB to save variables to a file?
A) `load()`
B) `save()`
C) `write()`
D) `store()`
Answer: B) `save()`

23. How would you load data from a `.mat` file in MATLAB?
A) `load('filename.mat')`
B) `read('filename.mat')`
C) `import('filename.mat')`
D) `open('filename.mat')`
Answer: A) `load('filename.mat')`

24. Which function is used to write data to a text file in MATLAB?
A) `fprintf()`
B) `write()`
C) `save()`
D) `fwrite()`
Answer: A) `fprintf()`

25. In C, which function is used to open a file for writing?
A) `open()`
B) `create()`
C) `fopen()`
D) `write()`
Answer: C) `fopen()`

4.1 Basic Plotting in MATLAB

1. Create a line plot of the sine function for values of x between 0 and 2π.
Answer:

```
x = 0:0.01:2*pi;
y = sin(x);
plot(x, y);
```

2. Write MATLAB code to plot a bar chart for the following data: x = [1, 2, 3, 4, 5], y = [10, 20, 30, 40, 50].
Answer:

```
x = [1, 2, 3, 4, 5];
y = [10, 20, 30, 40, 50];
bar(x, y);
```

3. Generate a scatter plot of 50 random data points with x and y values between 0 and 1.
Answer:

```
x = rand(1, 50);
y = rand(1, 50);
scatter(x, y);
```

4. Add x and y axis labels and a title to a sine wave plot.
Answer:

```
x = 0:0.01:2*pi;
y = sin(x);
plot(x, y);
xlabel('x');
ylabel('sin(x)');
title('Sine Wave');
```

5. Plot both sine and cosine curves on the same graph with appropriate labels and legends.
Answer:

```
x = 0:0.1:2*pi;
y1 = sin(x);
y2 = cos(x);
plot(x, y1, 'r', x, y2, 'b');
xlabel('x');
ylabel('y');
title('Sine and Cosine Waves');
legend('sin(x)', 'cos(x)');
```

4.2 Built-in Functions for Data Visualization

6. Use the `histogram` function to plot a histogram of 1000 random numbers generated from a normal distribution.
Answer:

```
data = randn(1, 1000);
histogram(data);
```

7. Plot a 3D surface plot of the function z = sin(x) * cos(y) over a grid of x and y values.
Answer:

```
 [x, y] = meshgrid(-5:0.1:5, -5:0.1:5);
z = sin(x) .* cos(y);
surf(x, y, z);
```

8. Generate a 3D mesh plot for the function z = x^2 + y^2.
Answer:

```
 [x, y] = meshgrid(-5:0.1:5, -5:0.1:5);
z = x.^2 + y.^2;
mesh(x, y, z);
```

9. Use the `plot3` function to plot a 3D line for the parametric equations x = t, y = t^2, z = t^3.
Answer:

```
t = -5:0.1:5;
x = t;
y = t.^2;
z = t.^3;
plot3(x, y, z);
```

10. Write MATLAB code to create a pie chart displaying the following values: [30, 40, 20, 10].
Answer:

```
data = [30, 40, 20, 10];
pie(data);
```

4.3 Generating Waveforms and Sound Replay

11. Generate and plot a sine wave with a frequency of 2 Hz for a time range of 0 to 1 second.
Answer:

```
t = 0:0.01:1;   % Time vector
f = 2;          % Frequency in Hz
```

```
y = sin(2*pi*f*t);   % Sine wave
plot(t, y);
xlabel('Time (seconds)');
ylabel('Amplitude');
title('Sine Wave with Frequency 2 Hz');
```

12. Generate a square wave with a frequency of 3 Hz and plot it.
Answer:

```
t = 0:0.01:1;   % Time vector
f = 3;           % Frequency in Hz
y = square(2*pi*f*t);   % Square wave
plot(t, y);
xlabel('Time (seconds)');
ylabel('Amplitude');
title('Square Wave with Frequency 3 Hz');
```

13. Generate a triangle wave with a frequency of 1 Hz and plot it.
Answer:

```
t = 0:0.01:1;   % Time vector
f = 1;           % Frequency in Hz
y = sawtooth(2*pi*f*t, 0.5);   % Triangle wave
plot(t, y);
xlabel('Time (seconds)');
ylabel('Amplitude');
title('Triangle Wave with Frequency 1 Hz');
```

14. Write MATLAB code to load and play an audio file named soundfile.wav.
Answer:

```
 [y, Fs] = audioread('soundfile.wav');   % Load audio file
sound(y, Fs);                            % Play the audio file
```

15. Generate and play a sine wave with a frequency of 5 Hz and a duration of 2 seconds.
Answer:

```
t = 0:0.01:2;   % Time vector for 2 seconds
f = 5;           % Frequency in Hz
y = sin(2*pi*f*t);   % Sine wave
sound(y, 100);   % Play the sine wave sound
```

CHAPTER 5: FUNCTIONS AND PROCEDURES IN MATLAB

5.1 Writing Functions in MATLAB

MATLAB functions are an integral part of programming, providing a structured way to organize and modularize your code. Functions allow you to encapsulate code into reusable blocks that can be called with different inputs, perform specific operations, and return outputs. Functions help in reducing redundancy, improving readability, and enhancing maintainability of code.

Let's break down the process of defining functions, passing input and output parameters, and understanding the syntax involved.

Function Definitions and Syntax

In MATLAB, functions are typically defined in separate files, with the function name being the same as the filename (with the `.m` extension). The general syntax to define a function is:

```
function [output1, output2] = functionName(input1, input2)
    % Function body
    % Perform calculations or operations
    output1 = input1 + input2;   % Example operation
    output2 = input1 * input2;   % Example operation
end
```

Breakdown of the Syntax:

- **function**: The `function` keyword indicates the start of a function definition. MATLAB recognizes this as a function definition.
- **[output1, output2]**: These are the output arguments. The function can return multiple outputs or just a single output. If the function returns multiple values, they are enclosed in square brackets `[ ]`.
- **functionName**: This is the name of the function. It must be the same as the name of the file. For example, if the function is `addNumbers`, the file should be named `addNumbers.m`.
- **(input1, input2)**: These are the input arguments. The values you provide for these parameters when calling the function are passed into the function for processing.

Example Function:

Here's an example of a simple function that adds two numbers:

```
function result = addNumbers(a, b)
    result = a + b;   % Adds the two input arguments
end
```

- This function is named `addNumbers` and takes two inputs (`a` and `b`), then returns their sum as `result`.

Calling the Function:

To call this function and obtain the result:

```
sum = addNumbers(5, 3);   % sum will be 8
disp(sum);   % Displays: 8
```

Here, 5 and 3 are passed as arguments to the `addNumbers` function, and the result is stored in the variable `sum`.

Input and Output Parameters

- **Input Parameters**: These are the variables or values that are passed to the function. When calling a function, the arguments you pass are assigned to the input parameters in the function definition.
- **Output Parameters**: These are the variables where the results of the function are returned. They appear before the = sign in the function definition.

Example Function with Multiple Outputs:

Here is a more complex example of a function that calculates both the sum and product of two numbers:

```
function [sum, product] = calcOperations(a, b)
    sum = a + b;          % Addition operation
    product = a * b;      % Multiplication operation
end
```

In this function:

- The function name is `calcOperations`.
- It takes two inputs: `a` and `b`.
- It returns two outputs: `sum` and `product`.

Calling the Function with Multiple Outputs:

To call the function and get both outputs:

```
 [aSum, aProduct] = calcOperations(3, 4);
disp(aSum);        % Displays: 7
disp(aProduct);    % Displays: 12
```

Here, the function returns both the sum (7) and product (12) of the input values 3 and 4. These outputs are captured by `aSum` and `aProduct`.

Key Points to Remember

1. **Function Name and Filename**: The function name in MATLAB must match the filename. For example, if your function is named `addNumbers`, the file must be named `addNumbers.m`.
2. **Multiple Outputs**: You can return multiple outputs from a function. If you have more than one output, they are returned in square brackets, like `[output1, output2]`.
3. **Return Values**: Functions return values when they are called. You can use the returned values for further calculations or simply display them.
4. **No Need for Explicit Data Types**: MATLAB is dynamically typed, meaning you don't need to specify the type of the inputs or outputs. The type is determined based on the data passed into the function.

Examples of Calling Functions with Different Numbers of Outputs

- **Single Output**:

  If you call the function and only care about one of the outputs, you can omit the others:

  ```
  aSum = calcOperations(3, 4);   % Only captures the sum (7)
  disp(aSum);   % Displays: 7
  ```

- **Multiple Outputs**:

  If you want both the sum and the product:

  ```
  [sum, product] = calcOperations(3, 4);   % Captures both outputs
  disp(sum);   % Displays: 7
  disp(product);   % Displays: 12
  ```

- **Ignoring Outputs**:

  If you only care about one output and want to ignore the others, you can use a tilde (~) to ignore specific outputs:

  ```
  [sum, ~] = calcOperations(3, 4);   % Only captures sum and ignores product
  disp(sum);   % Displays: 7
  ```

5.2 M-files: Scripts and Functions

In MATLAB, code is typically written in files with the `.m` extension. There are two primary types of `.m` files: **scripts** and **functions**. Both serve different purposes and have distinct behaviors in MATLAB programming. Let's explore their structure, use, and the key differences between them.

Structure of M-files and Their Uses

1. Scripts:

- **Definition**: A **script** is a sequence of MATLAB commands saved in a `.m` file. It is essentially a batch of commands that MATLAB executes in order, one after the other. Scripts do not accept input arguments or return output values. They operate directly on variables in the **MATLAB workspace**.
- **Key Characteristics**:
  - Scripts do not have input or output parameters.
  - They manipulate or work with the variables in the workspace, meaning they do not encapsulate any data.
  - Scripts are useful when you want to execute a series of commands without the need for reusable or modular code.

Example of a Script:

Let's say you want to add two numbers and display the result.

```
% script.m
x = 5;            % Assign value to x
y = 10;           % Assign value to y
result = x + y;   % Perform addition
disp(result);     % Display the result
```

- **How it works**:
  - The script sets x and y to 5 and 10 respectively, performs an addition, and then displays the result.
  - To run this script, you simply type `script` (or press the Run button in MATLAB). MATLAB will execute all the lines of the script in order.
- **Usage**:
  - Scripts are good for quick, sequential tasks like performing calculations or generating simple plots.
  - They are not ideal for modular or reusable code since they don't allow you to pass inputs or return outputs.

---

2. Functions:

- **Definition**: A **function** in MATLAB is a separate `.m` file that starts with a `function` keyword. Functions are used to encapsulate reusable code logic, and unlike scripts, they **accept input arguments** and **return output values**. Functions allow you to organize your code in a more structured and modular way, making it easier to reuse and maintain.
- **Key Characteristics**:
    - ○ Functions can take input arguments and return output arguments.
    - ○ They are stored in their own files, and the file name must match the function name.
    - ○ Functions operate within their own scope and cannot directly modify variables in the workspace unless explicitly returned as outputs.

Example of a Function:

Consider a function that calculates the area of a circle given its radius.

```
% calcArea.m
function area = calcArea(radius)
    area = pi * radius^2; % Calculate area of a circle
end
```

- **How it works**:
    - ○ The function `calcArea` takes one input parameter (`radius`) and calculates the area of the circle using the formula πr^2.
    - ○ To use this function, you would call it with a specific radius value, and it would return the area.

Calling the Function:

```
radius = 5;            % Assign a value to radius
area = calcArea(radius);  % Call the function to calculate area
disp(area);            % Display the area
```

- **Output**: The area of the circle is displayed in the command window.
- **Usage**: Functions are ideal for creating modular code that can be reused multiple times with different inputs, improving code clarity and reusability.

Writing Reusable Functions (MATLAB vs C)

Both MATLAB and C allow for the creation of reusable functions, but they differ in syntax, typing, and function structure. Below is a comparison of writing reusable functions in both languages:

MATLAB:

- **Dynamic Typing**: MATLAB is dynamically typed, meaning you don't need to specify the data type of the input or output parameters in the function. The function can accept any type of data (numeric, string, etc.) and MATLAB automatically handles the types during runtime.
- **Function Definition Example**:

```
function result = multiply(a, b)
    result = a * b;
end
```

- **Function Call**:

```
product = multiply(4, 5);  % This works even if a and b are of
different types
disp(product);  % Displays: 20
```

- **Characteristics**:
    - You don't need to declare variable types explicitly.
    - MATLAB automatically handles the data types.
    - Functions are easy to write and flexible, making it suitable for mathematical and scientific applications.

C:

- **Static Typing**: C is statically typed, meaning you must explicitly declare the types of all variables and function arguments. The types of inputs and outputs are fixed when the function is defined.
- **Function Definition Example**:

```
int multiply(int a, int b) {
    return a * b;
}
```

- **Function Call**:

```
int result = multiply(4, 5);  // Type of arguments and return value is
explicit
printf("%d", result);  // Displays: 20
```

- **Characteristics**:
    - You need to declare the data type of input and output variables.
    - C is more structured but requires more lines of code for variable declarations.
    - Functions in C are more efficient in terms of memory and performance but are more complex to write compared to MATLAB functions.

Key Differences Between MATLAB and C Functions:

Feature	MATLAB	C
Typing	Dynamic (no need to specify types)	Static (types must be defined)
Function Declaration	No type required for inputs/outputs	Must specify input/output types
Syntax Simplicity	Simplified, concise code	Requires more verbose code for type declarations
Memory Management	Handled by MATLAB	Explicit memory management needed
Performance	Easier to write, but slower	Faster execution, more control over resources

5.3 Formatted Console Input/Output

In MATLAB, interacting with users and presenting data in a formatted way is an essential part of developing user-friendly applications. MATLAB provides several built-in functions for **formatted input and output**, which help collect input from the user and display results in a clear and organized manner. Let's break down the key functions and techniques used for formatted console input/output.

---

1. User Input with `input`, `menu`, and `fprintf`

a. `input` Function:

The `input` function prompts the user for input and stores the entered value in a variable. It can also display a custom message to guide the user.

- **Syntax**:

```
variable = input('Prompt message: ');
```

- **How it works**:
  - `input` pauses the program and waits for the user to enter data.
  - The input can be a number, string, or any other data type depending on the user's input.
- **Example**:

```
x = input('Enter a number: ');  % User input is stored in x
disp(['You entered: ', num2str(x)]);  % Display the entered number
```

- **Explanation**:
  - ○ The prompt `'Enter a number: '` appears in the MATLAB console, asking the user to input a number.
  - ○ `num2str(x)` converts the number into a string to concatenate with the text and display it using `disp()`.
- **Output**: If the user inputs 5, the program will display:

```
You entered: 5
```

---

b. `menu` Function:

The `menu` function creates a simple graphical menu with multiple options. The user can select an option from the list, and MATLAB returns the index number of the chosen option.

- **Syntax**:

```
choice = menu('Title', 'Option1', 'Option2', 'Option3', ...);
```

- **How it works**:
  - ○ The `menu` function displays a pop-up menu with the given options.
  - ○ The function returns an integer value corresponding to the selected option (starting from 1 for the first option).
- **Example**:

```
choice = menu('Select an option', 'Option 1', 'Option 2', 'Option 3');
disp(['You chose option ', num2str(choice)]);
```

- **Explanation**:
  - ○ The menu will show three options for the user to choose from.
  - ○ The selected option is returned as an integer (1 for "Option 1", 2 for "Option 2", etc.) and displayed using `disp()`.
- **Output**: If the user selects "Option 2", the program will display:

```
You chose option 2
```

---

c. `fprintf` Function:

The `fprintf` function is used to output formatted text and variables to the MATLAB console (or a file). This function gives you control over how the output is displayed, including the number of decimal places, alignment, and other formatting options.

- **Syntax**:

```
fprintf('Text with format specifiers', variable1, variable2, ...);
```

- **How it works**:
  - o The `fprintf` function uses **format specifiers** (like `%f`, `%d`, etc.) to determine how variables should be formatted when displayed.
  - o You can specify the number of decimal places for floating-point numbers, and also align the text and values within a specified width.
- **Example**:

```
x = 5;
fprintf('The value of x is: %.2f\n', x);  % Formats x to two decimal
places
```

- **Explanation**:
  - o The `%.2f` format specifier formats the floating-point number `x` to **two decimal places**.
  - o `\n` inserts a newline character at the end of the output.
- **Output**:

```
The value of x is: 5.00
```

2. Formatting Output: `sprintf` and `fprintf`

a. `sprintf` Function:

The `sprintf` function is similar to `fprintf`, but instead of printing the result to the console, it returns the formatted string as an output. This can be useful when you want to store the formatted string in a variable for further processing or display later.

- **Syntax**:

```
formatted_string = sprintf('Text with format specifiers', variable1,
variable2, ...);
```

- **How it works**:
  - o The `sprintf` function does not display anything on the console; it **returns** the formatted string.
  - o You can store this string in a variable and use it later in the program.
- **Example**:

```
str = sprintf('The result is: %.3f', 3.14159);  % Store formatted
string
disp(str);  % Display the formatted string
```

- **Explanation**:
  - o `%.3f` formats the number `3.14159` to **three decimal places**.
  - o The resulting string is stored in the variable `str` and then displayed using `disp()`.
- **Output**:

```
The result is: 3.142
```

b. `fprintf` Function (Console Output):

As mentioned earlier, `fprintf` outputs a formatted string directly to the console or a file. It is useful when you want to print formatted results directly, especially in interactive scripts or when writing output to log files.

- **Example**:

```
fprintf('Value of pi: %.4f\n', pi);  % Output pi to four decimal places
```

- **Explanation**:
  - o `%.4f` formats the value of `pi` to **four decimal places**.
  - o `\n` ensures the output is followed by a newline.
- **Output**:

```
Value of pi: 3.1416
```

3. Format Specifiers in MATLAB

MATLAB's `sprintf` and `fprintf` functions support a variety of format specifiers to control how numbers, strings, and other data types are displayed. Some commonly used format specifiers are:

- `%f`: For **floating-point numbers** (e.g., `3.14`)
- `%d`: For **integers** (e.g., `42`)
- `%s`: For **strings** (e.g., `'Hello, World!'`)
- `%.2f`: For **floating-point numbers rounded to two decimal places** (e.g., `3.14` becomes `3.14`)
- `%e`: For **scientific notation** (e.g., `3.1416` becomes `3.1416e+00`)

Examples of Format Specifiers:

1. **For a floating-point number with 2 decimal places**:

```
fprintf('Value with 2 decimals: %.2f\n', 3.14159);  % Output: 3.14
```

2. **For an integer**:

```
fprintf('Integer value: %d\n', 42);  % Output: 42
```

3. **For a string**:

```
fprintf('Greeting: %s\n', 'Hello, MATLAB!');  % Output: Hello, MATLAB!
```

25 multiple-choice questions (MCQs)

5.1 Writing Functions in MATLAB

Function Definitions and Syntax

1. **What is the correct syntax to define a function in MATLAB?** a)
   ```
   function_name(output, input) {}
   ```
   b) `function output = function_name(input)`
   c) `function (output, input) = function_name`
   d) `output = function_name(input, input)`

   Answer: b) `function output = function_name(input)`

2. **In MATLAB, the function definition must start with the keyword:** a) `define`
   b) `function`
   c) `def`
   d) `create`

   Answer: b) `function`

3. **When calling a function in MATLAB, what is returned if there is no output variable?** a) `0`
   b) The function name
   c) An error
   d) The workspace variable

   Answer: c) An error

Input and Output Parameters

4. **Which of the following is true when passing parameters to a MATLAB function?** a) All input variables must be strings
   b) Output variables are optional
   c) MATLAB automatically checks for parameter types
   d) Input parameters can only be integers

   Answer: b) Output variables are optional

5. **What happens if you do not assign the function output to any variable?** a) The function still executes, but the result is not stored
   b) MATLAB throws an error
   c) It returns a default value
   d) The program halts

   Answer: a) The function still executes, but the result is not stored

6. **Which of the following MATLAB function outputs will return multiple values?** a) `sum`

   b) `mean`

   c) `calcOperations`

   d) `sin`

   Answer: c) `calcOperations`

5.2 M-files: Scripts and Functions

Structure of M-files and Their Uses

7. **What is the difference between a script and a function in MATLAB?** a) A script can return values; a function cannot

   b) A function can accept input arguments; a script cannot

   c) A script is used for plotting, while a function is used for calculations

   d) Scripts do not have a `.m` file extension

   Answer: b) A function can accept input arguments; a script cannot

8. **Which type of MATLAB file allows you to store and execute a series of commands without accepting input or returning output?** a) Function

   b) Class

   c) Script

   d) Package

   Answer: c) Script

9. **Where are the variables used in a script stored in MATLAB?** a) In the function workspace

   b) In the global workspace

   c) In the workspace that was active when the script was run

   d) In a temporary variable location

   Answer: c) In the workspace that was active when the script was run

10. **Which of the following is a correct example of a script in MATLAB?** a) `function result = calculateSum(x, y)`

    b) `x = 10; y = 5; disp(x + y);`

    c) `function calculateSum(x, y)`

    d) `result = calculateSum(3, 7);`

Answer: b) `x = 10; y = 5; disp(x + y);`

Writing Reusable Functions (MATLAB vs C)

11. **How does function writing in MATLAB differ from C?** a) MATLAB requires explicit data type declarations for variables, unlike C
    b) Functions in MATLAB are more rigid in terms of input/output types
    c) MATLAB functions are dynamically typed, while C requires explicit type declarations
    d) There is no difference in how functions are written

Answer: c) MATLAB functions are dynamically typed, while C requires explicit type declarations

12. **What must be specified at the start of a function definition in C?** a) The output variables
    b) The function name only
    c) The return type of the function
    d) Input arguments only

Answer: c) The return type of the function

13. **In MATLAB, which of the following is true when calling a function with an unspecified return type?** a) An error is generated
    b) MATLAB assigns a default type to the output
    c) The output is stored in the base workspace
    d) The function will still execute, but no result will be stored

Answer: d) The function will still execute, but no result will be stored

14. **In C, the return type of a function must be explicitly defined. What is the equivalent in MATLAB?** a) MATLAB always returns a double-precision value
    b) MATLAB can return values without specifying types in advance
    c) MATLAB uses pointers for function return
    d) MATLAB requires you to specify return types as well

Answer: b) MATLAB can return values without specifying types in advance

15. **Which of the following is a reusable function in MATLAB?** a) A script that saves data to a file
    b) A function that calculates the area of a circle
    c) A series of `disp` statements
    d) A plot command

Answer: b) A function that calculates the area of a circle

5.3 Formatted Console Input/Output

User Input with `input`, `menu`, and `fprintf`

16. **What does the `input` function do in MATLAB?** a) It prompts the user to choose an option from a menu
    b) It prints a formatted message to the console
    c) It collects user input from the command window
    d) It returns output to the console

Answer: c) It collects user input from the command window

17. **Which function is used to create a menu for the user to choose from a list of options in MATLAB?** a) `input`
    b) `fprintf`
    c) `menu`
    d) `select`

Answer: c) `menu`

18. **Which of the following is true about the `fprintf` function in MATLAB?** a) It accepts input from the user and displays it
    b) It displays formatted output to the console or a file
    c) It saves user input to a variable
    d) It formats the output for future use without printing it

Answer: b) It displays formatted output to the console or a file

19. **What is the main difference between `fprintf` and `sprintf`?** a) `fprintf` writes to a file, while `sprintf` outputs to the console
    b) `fprintf` stores the result in a variable, while `sprintf` displays the result
    c) `fprintf` directly prints to the console, while `sprintf` stores the result in a variable
    d) `fprintf` is used for numeric data, while `sprintf` is used for text

Answer: c) `fprintf` directly prints to the console, while `sprintf` stores the result in a variable

20. **How do you format a floating-point number to two decimal places in MATLAB?** a) `sprintf('%.2f', num)`
    b) `fprintf('%.2f', num)`
    c) `sprintf('%2f', num)`
    d) Both a and b

Answer: d) Both a and b

Formatting Output: `sprintf` and `fprintf`

21. **Which of the following format specifiers is used to print an integer in MATLAB?** a) `%s`
    b) `%f`
    c) `%d`
    d) `%e`

Answer: c) `%d`

22. **What is the result of the following code?**

```
x = 3.14159;
fprintf('Value: %.3f\n', x);
```

a) `Value: 3.14`
b) `Value: 3.141`
c) `Value: 3.142`
d) `Value: 3.14159`

Answer: c) `Value: 3.142`

23. **Which function is used to output formatted data directly to the console in MATLAB?** a) `input`
    b) `disp`
    c) `fprintf`
    d) `sprintf`

Answer: c) `fprintf`

24. **What does the `\n` character do in `fprintf`?** a) Starts a new line in the console output
    b) Replaces a space with a newline
    c) Adds a numeric value
    d) Formats the number as scientific notation

Answer: a) Starts a new line in the console output

25. **Which format specifier would you use to display a string in MATLAB?** a) `%f`
    b) `%d`
    c) `%s`
    d) `%e`

Answer: c) `%s`

5.1 Writing Functions in MATLAB

Function Definitions and Syntax

1. **Question:** Write a MATLAB function `addNumbers` that takes two input arguments `a` and `b`, and returns their sum.
   o **Answer:**

```
function result = addNumbers(a, b)
    result = a + b;
end
```

2. **Question:** Write a function `subtractNumbers` that accepts two arguments `a` and `b`, and returns the result of `a - b`.
   - **Answer:**

```
function result = subtractNumbers(a, b)
    result = a - b;
end
```

3. **Question:** Create a MATLAB function `calculateRectangleArea` that takes the length and width of a rectangle as input and returns the area.
   - **Answer:**

```
function area = calculateRectangleArea(length, width)
    area = length * width;
end
```

4. **Question:** Write a function `calculateCircleArea` that accepts the radius of a circle and returns the area. Use the constant `pi` in the calculation.
   - **Answer:**

```
function area = calculateCircleArea(radius)
    area = pi * radius^2;
end
```

5. **Question:** Write a function `maxOfTwo` that takes two numbers as input and returns the maximum value.
   - **Answer:**

```
function maxVal = maxOfTwo(a, b)
    maxVal = max(a, b);
end
```

Input and Output Parameters

6. **Question:** Write a function `areaAndPerimeter` that accepts the length and width of a rectangle and returns both the area and perimeter.
   - **Answer:**

```
function [area, perimeter] = areaAndPerimeter(length, width)
    area = length * width;
    perimeter = 2 * (length + width);
end
```

7. **Question:** Create a function `getSumAndProduct` that takes two input arguments and returns their sum and product in a single output (a 2-element vector).
   - **Answer:**

```
function result = getSumAndProduct(a, b)
```

```
        result = [a + b, a * b];
    end
```

8. **Question:** Write a function `reverseString` that takes a string as input and returns the reversed string.
    - **Answer:**

```
function reversed = reverseString(str)
    reversed = flip(str);
end
```

9. **Question:** Create a function `convertToFahrenheit` that converts a temperature in Celsius to Fahrenheit. The function should return the Fahrenheit value.
    - **Answer:**

```
fahrenheit = convertToFahrenheit(celsius)
    fahrenheit = (celsius * 9/5) + 32;
end
```

10. **Question:** Write a function `isEven` that takes a number as input and returns true if the number is even and false otherwise.
    - **Answer:**

```
function result = isEven(n)
    result = mod(n, 2) == 0;
end
```

5.2 M-files: Scripts and Functions

Structure of M-files and Their Uses

11. **Question:** Create a script that defines a vector `v = [1, 2, 3, 4, 5]` and prints the sum of all elements in the vector.
    - **Answer:**

```
v = [1, 2, 3, 4, 5];
totalSum = sum(v);
disp(totalSum);
```

12. **Question:** Write a script that takes two numbers from the user, calculates their sum, and displays the result.
    - **Answer:**

```
a = input('Enter the first number: ');
b = input('Enter the second number: ');
result = a + b;
disp(['The sum is: ', num2str(result)]);
```

13. **Question:** Write a script that creates a matrix A = [1, 2; 3, 4] and calculates the determinant of the matrix.
   - **Answer:**

```
A = [1, 2; 3, 4];
det_A = det(A);
disp(['Determinant of A is: ', num2str(det_A)]);
```

14. **Question:** Create a script that generates a random matrix of size 3x3 and displays the maximum value from the matrix.
   - **Answer:**

```
A = rand(3, 3);
maxVal = max(A(:));
disp(['Maximum value: ', num2str(maxVal)]);
```

Writing Reusable Functions (MATLAB vs C)

15. **Question:** Write a MATLAB function `multiply` that accepts two numbers as inputs and returns their product. Compare this to a C version of the function.
   - **MATLAB Version:**

```
function result = multiply(a, b)
    result = a * b;
end
```

   - **C Version:**

```
#include <stdio.h>
int multiply(int a, int b) {
    return a * b;
}
int main() {
    int result = multiply(2, 3);
    printf("The result is: %d\n", result);
    return 0;
}
```

5.3 Formatted Console Input/Output

User Input with input, menu, and fprintf

16. **Question:** Write a script that asks the user to input their name and age and then displays a message with their name and age.
   - **Answer:**

```
name = input('Enter your name: ', 's');
age = input('Enter your age: ');
disp(['Hello, ', name, '! You are ', num2str(age), ' years old.']);
```

17. **Question:** Create a script that displays a menu with three options and stores the user's choice in a variable.
   - **Answer:**

```
choice = menu('Select an option', 'Option 1', 'Option 2', 'Option 3');
disp(['You chose option ', num2str(choice)]);
```

18. **Question:** Write a script that takes an input number x from the user and then prints it using `fprintf`, formatted to 2 decimal places.
   - **Answer:**

```
x = input('Enter a number: ');
fprintf('The number is: %.2f\n', x);
```

Formatting Output: sprintf and fprintf

19. **Question:** Use `sprintf` to format a number with 3 decimal places and store it in a variable. Display the formatted result.
   - **Answer:**

```
num = 3.14159;
str = sprintf('The value of pi is: %.3f', num);
disp(str);
```

20. **Question:** Write a script that takes an integer from the user and prints the formatted output using `fprintf`.
   - **Answer:**

```
n = input('Enter an integer: ');
fprintf('The entered integer is: %d\n', n);
```

21. **Question:** Create a script that asks the user for their first and last name, then prints a message using `fprintf`.
   - **Answer:**

```
firstName = input('Enter your first name: ', 's');
lastName = input('Enter your last name: ', 's');
fprintf('Hello, %s %s!\n', firstName, lastName);
```

22. **Question:** Use `fprintf` to display the result of multiplying two numbers, formatted to 1 decimal place.
   - **Answer:**

```
num1 = 5.23;
num2 = 3.12;
result = num1 * num2;
fprintf('The result is: %.1f\n', result);
```

23. **Question:** Write a script that takes a decimal number as input and prints it formatted as a percentage using `fprintf`.
   o **Answer:**

```
decimal = input('Enter a decimal number: ');
fprintf('The number as a percentage is: %.2f%%\n', decimal * 100);
```

24. **Question:** Create a script that takes two integers as input and prints their sum, difference, and product using `fprintf`.
   o **Answer:**

```
a = input('Enter the first number: ');
b = input('Enter the second number: ');
fprintf('Sum: %d\n', a + b);
fprintf('Difference: %d\n', a - b);
fprintf('Product: %d\n', a * b);
```

25. **Question:** Use `sprintf` to create a formatted string that includes a variable and display the result.
   o **Answer:**

```
radius = 7;
str = sprintf('The radius of the circle is %.2f units.', radius);
disp(str);
```

CHAPTER 6: STRING HANDLING AND TEXT OPERATIONS

6.1 String Handling in MATLAB

MATLAB provides powerful tools for creating, manipulating, and modifying strings. Strings in MATLAB can be handled using either **character arrays** (traditional approach) or **string arrays** (newer and more flexible method introduced in MATLAB R2016b). Each of these has its own set of functionalities that you can utilize depending on your task.

Creating and Manipulating Strings

1. Character Arrays

A character array in MATLAB is a collection of individual characters, each treated as a separate element in an array. Character arrays are enclosed in single quotes (' ').

- **Creating a Character Array**: A string can be created by assigning it directly to a variable. Each character is stored as an individual element in the array.

  Example:

  ```
  str = 'Hello, World!';  % Create a character array
  disp(str);  % Displays 'Hello, World!'
  ```

  Here, str is a character array containing the text Hello, World!. Each character is stored individually, and the size of the array is equal to the number of characters.

- **Manipulating Character Arrays**: You can manipulate character arrays using various functions.

  Example:

  ```
  str = 'MATLAB';  % Character array
  len = length(str);  % Returns the number of characters in the string
  disp(len);  % Displays '6'

  % Converting to uppercase
  upperStr = upper(str);  % Converts 'MATLAB' to 'MATLAB'
  disp(upperStr);  % Displays 'MATLAB'

  % Converting to lowercase
  lowerStr = lower(str);  % Converts 'MATLAB' to 'matlab'
  disp(lowerStr);  % Displays 'matlab'
  ```

2. String Arrays

String arrays are a more modern way of working with strings. They are created using **double quotes** (" "), which makes them more versatile and easier to manipulate than character arrays.

- **Creating a String Array**: Example:

```
str = "Hello, World!";  % Create a string array
disp(str);  % Displays "Hello, World!"
```

Unlike character arrays, string arrays are more flexible and can hold multiple strings in one variable.

- **Manipulating String Arrays**: String arrays allow for similar operations like converting to uppercase or lowercase, but the functions are specific to string arrays, such as `upper`, `lower`, `replace`, etc.

Example:

```
str = "MATLAB";
len = strlength(str);  % Returns the number of characters in the string
disp(len);  % Displays '6'

% Convert string to upper case
upperStr = upper(str);
disp(upperStr);  % Displays 'MATLAB'

% Convert string to lower case
lowerStr = lower(str);
disp(lowerStr);  % Displays 'matlab'
```

Concatenating and Modifying Strings

1. Concatenating Strings

Concatenating strings means joining two or more strings together. MATLAB offers different ways to concatenate strings depending on the type of strings you are using (character arrays or string arrays).

- **Concatenating String Arrays**: In string arrays, concatenation is performed using the + operator.

Example:

```
str1 = "Hello";
str2 = "World";
combined = str1 + " " + str2;  % Concatenates "Hello World"
disp(combined);  % Displays "Hello World"
```

- **Concatenating Character Arrays**: In character arrays, concatenation is done using the `strcat` function, which appends one string to another.

Example:

```
str1 = 'Hello';
str2 = 'World';
combined = strcat(str1, ' ', str2);  % Concatenates 'Hello World'
disp(combined);  % Displays 'Hello World'
```

2. Modifying Strings

Modifying strings involves changing specific parts of the string or replacing parts of the string with other content. In MATLAB, you can modify strings using indexing or by using string manipulation functions like `replace`.

- **Modifying Character Arrays**: For character arrays, you can access specific positions within the string and change individual characters.

Example:

```
str = 'Hello World';
str(7:11) = 'MATLAB';  % Replaces 'World' with 'MATLAB'
disp(str);  % Displays 'Hello MATLAB'
```

Here, `str(7:11)` refers to the characters from index 7 to index 11 of the string, which are replaced by the new string `'MATLAB'`.

- **Modifying String Arrays**: In string arrays, you can use the `replace` function to replace a substring with another string.

Example:

```
str = "Hello World";
str = replace(str, "World", "MATLAB");  % Replaces 'World' with
'MATLAB'
disp(str);  % Displays 'Hello MATLAB'
```

Here, the `replace` function searches for the substring `"World"` and replaces it with `"MATLAB"`. This is a flexible way to modify parts of a string.

Key Functions for String Manipulation

Here are some important MATLAB functions used for string handling:

1. **length**: Returns the number of characters in a character array.

- o Example: `len = length('MATLAB');` returns 6.
2. **strlength**: Similar to `length`, but works specifically for string arrays.
   - o Example: `len = strlength("MATLAB");` returns 6.
3. **upper**: Converts all characters in a string or character array to uppercase.
   - o Example: `upper('hello')` returns `'HELLO'`.
4. **lower**: Converts all characters in a string or character array to lowercase.
   - o Example: `lower('HELLO')` returns `'hello'`.
5. **strcat**: Concatenates multiple character arrays.
   - o Example: `strcat('Hello', ' ', 'World')` returns `'Hello World'`.
6. **replace**: Replaces occurrences of a substring within a string or string array.
   - o Example: `replace("Hello World", "World", "MATLAB")` returns `"Hello MATLAB"`.
7. **strfind**: Finds the indices of a substring within a string or character array.
   - o Example: `strfind('Hello World', 'World')` returns 7.
8. **strcmp**: Compares two strings for equality, returning 1 (true) if they are the same, and 0 (false) if they are different.
   - o Example: `strcmp('MATLAB', 'matlab')` returns 0.
9. **sprintf**: Formats data into a string. This is similar to `fprintf`, but the result is stored in a string variable instead of being printed.
   - o Example: `str = sprintf('Value: %.2f', 3.14159)` returns `'Value: 3.14'`.

6.2 File Operations: Reading and Writing Text Files

MATLAB provides a set of robust functions for working with files. These functions allow you to open, read, write, and close files, making it easy to store and retrieve data for your applications. Understanding how to use file operations in MATLAB can significantly enhance your ability to manage data, automate tasks, and process external files.

Using `fopen`, `fclose`, `fread`, `fwrite`

1. Opening a File with `fopen`

The **fopen** function in MATLAB is used to open a file for reading, writing, or appending data. It returns a **file identifier** (`fid`), which is used in subsequent file operations.

- **Syntax:**

```
fid = fopen(filename, permission);
```

   - o **filename**: The name of the file you wish to open.
   - o **permission**: Specifies the type of access required. Common options include:
     - ▪ `'r'`: Open the file for **reading** (the file must exist).

- 'w': Open the file for **writing** (creates a new file or overwrites an existing file).
- 'a': Open the file for **appending** data (adds to the end of the file).
- 'r+': Open the file for **reading and writing**.

If the file cannot be opened, fopen returns -1, indicating an error.

Example:

```
fid = fopen('example.txt', 'w');  % Open a file for writing
if fid == -1
    error('File could not be opened');
end
```

In this example, we try to open a file named example.txt in write mode ('w'). If the file cannot be opened (e.g., due to permissions or non-existence), MATLAB throws an error.

2. Reading from a File with fread

The **fread** function reads binary data from a file. It's commonly used to handle non-text files or when binary data is required. However, for reading text files, functions like fgets, fscanf, or textscan are often more suitable.

- **Syntax**:

  ```
  data = fread(fid, size, precision);
  ```

  - **fid**: The file identifier returned by fopen.
  - **size**: Specifies the number of elements to read.
  - **precision**: Specifies the data type to be read (e.g., 'char', 'int32').

For text files, you typically use **fgets** (reads a line of text) or **fscanf** (reads formatted data).

Example:

```
fid = fopen('example.txt', 'r');  % Open the file for reading
content = fread(fid, '*char')';   % Read file content as characters
fclose(fid);  % Close the file
disp(content);  % Display the content read from the file
```

Here, fread(fid, '*char') reads the content of the file as characters and converts them into a string. The fclose function is used to close the file after reading.

3. Writing to a File with fwrite

The **fwrite** function is used to write binary data to a file. This is suitable for non-text files, but for text-based files, you should use **fprintf**.

- **Syntax:**

```
fwrite(fid, data);
```

  - ○ **fid**: The file identifier.
  - ○ **data**: The data to write to the file.

Example:

```
fid = fopen('output.txt', 'w');   % Open the file for writing
fwrite(fid, 'This is a test.');
fclose(fid);   % Close the file
```

In this example, fwrite is used to write the text This is a test. into the file output.txt. Note that **fwrite** is generally used for binary data; for writing formatted text, **fprintf** is preferred.

---

4. Closing a File with fclose

The **fclose** function is used to close a file after reading or writing to it. It is essential to always close files to free up system resources.

- **Syntax:**

```
fclose(fid);
```

  - ○ **fid**: The file identifier.

Example:

```
fclose(fid);   % Close the file
```

After performing any file operation (reading, writing), it is important to close the file using fclose to ensure the data is saved properly and the file is released for other programs or operations.

MATLAB vs C for File I/O

MATLAB simplifies file I/O operations with built-in functions that are designed to handle both text and binary files with minimal effort. Functions like fopen, fclose, fread, fwrite, `fprintf`, `fscanf`, and `fgets` are all designed to be user-friendly, making MATLAB more efficient for data processing tasks.

In contrast, C requires more manual handling of file operations, such as managing file pointers, checking for errors, and specifying formats explicitly. C provides similar functions (`fopen`, `fclose`, `fread`, `fwrite`, `fprintf`, `fscanf`, `fgets`), but the process is generally more verbose and less abstracted than in MATLAB.

Example in C:

```c
#include <stdio.h>

int main() {
    FILE *file = fopen("example.txt", "w");  // Open file for writing
    if (file == NULL) {
        printf("Error opening file.\n");
        return 1;
    }
    fprintf(file, "Hello, World!");  // Write text to file
    fclose(file);  // Close the file
    return 0;
}
```

In C, you must explicitly check whether the file was opened successfully (e.g., by checking if `file` is `NULL`), and you need to handle more granular error checking. This manual process offers more control but also increases the complexity of the code.

6.3 Sorting and Searching Text Data

Sorting and searching are fundamental operations in data analysis, and MATLAB provides powerful tools to perform these tasks efficiently. Whether you're dealing with numerical data, text data, or a combination of both, MATLAB has built-in functions that simplify sorting and searching operations.

Sorting Arrays and Lists in MATLAB

MATLAB provides several functions to sort arrays and lists. Sorting is often useful in data analysis for organizing data, finding trends, or preparing data for further analysis.

1. Sorting Numerical Arrays

The most commonly used function for sorting numerical data is `sort`. By default, `sort` arranges the elements of an array in **ascending order**. You can specify the `'descend'` flag to sort in **descending order** instead.

- **Syntax**:

```
sortedArray = sort(array);  % Sort in ascending order
sortedArray = sort(array, 'descend');  % Sort in descending order
```

- **Example**:

```
A = [5, 2, 8, 3];
sortedA = sort(A);  % Sorts in ascending order: [2, 3, 5, 8]
sortedDescendA = sort(A, 'descend');  % Sorts in descending order: [8,
5, 3, 2]
disp(sortedA);
disp(sortedDescendA);
```

In this example:

- `sort(A)` sorts the array A in ascending order.
- `sort(A, 'descend')` sorts the array in descending order.

2. Sorting String Arrays

You can also sort string arrays in MATLAB, and the strings are compared **lexicographically** (alphabetically). The sorting is based on the ASCII or Unicode values of the characters.

- **Syntax**:

```
sortedStrArray = sort(strArray);
```

- **Example**:

```
strArray = ["apple", "orange", "banana", "grape"];
sortedStrArray = sort(strArray);  % Sorts alphabetically
disp(sortedStrArray);
```

In this example:

- `sort(strArray)` sorts the array of strings alphabetically, returning the sorted string array.

The result will be:

```
banana    grape    orange    apple
```

Implementing Search Algorithms in MATLAB

Searching is a fundamental operation in data analysis that allows you to find specific elements in an array. MATLAB provides several search algorithms, including **linear search** and **binary search**, depending on whether the array is sorted.

1. Linear Search

A **linear search** is a simple algorithm that checks each element of an array sequentially to find the target element. It is useful for unsorted arrays but is inefficient for large datasets because it checks every element until it finds the target.

- **Syntax**:

```
index = linearSearch(arr, target);
```

- **Example**:

```
function index = linearSearch(arr, target)
    index = -1;  % Default value if target is not found
    for i = 1:length(arr)
        if arr(i) == target
            index = i;  % Return the index of the target
            return;
        end
    end
end
```

Usage:

```
arr = [5, 2, 8, 3];
target = 8;
index = linearSearch(arr, target);  % Returns 3 (index of 8)
disp(index);
```

In this example:

- The function `linearSearch` takes an array `arr` and a target value `target` as inputs.
- It iterates through each element of the array until it finds the target value. If the target is found, the index of the target element is returned. Otherwise, it returns -1.

For the given array [5, 2, 8, 3] and target 8, the function will return the index 3, because 8 is found at the third position.

2. Binary Search

A **binary search** is a more efficient search algorithm but requires the array to be **sorted**. It works by repeatedly dividing the search interval in half. If the target value is smaller than the middle element, the search continues in the left half; otherwise, it continues in the right half. This algorithm is much faster than a linear search for large sorted datasets.

- **Syntax**:

```
index = binarySearch(arr, target);
```

- **Example**:

```
function index = binarySearch(arr, target)
    arr = sort(arr);   % Ensure the array is sorted
    left = 1;
    right = length(arr);
    while left <= right
        mid = floor((left + right) / 2);
        if arr(mid) == target
            index = mid;
            return;
        elseif arr(mid) < target
            left = mid + 1;
        else
            right = mid - 1;
        end
    end
    index = -1;   % Target not found
end
```

Usage:

```
arr = [1, 3, 5, 7, 9];
target = 5;
index = binarySearch(arr, target);   % Returns 3 (index of 5)
disp(index);
```

In this example:

- The `binarySearch` function first ensures the array is sorted by calling `sort(arr)`.
- It then initializes the `left` and `right` pointers to define the search range.
- The search continues by narrowing the range in half until the target is found or the range is empty.
- If the target is found, the function returns the index of the target. If not, it returns `-1`.

For the sorted array `[1, 3, 5, 7, 9]` and target 5, the function will return the index 3, because 5 is located at the third position in the sorted array.

25 multiple-choice questions (MCQs)

6.1 String Handling in MATLAB

1. Which of the following is the correct syntax to create a string in MATLAB?

A) `str = 'Hello';`
B) `str = ["Hello"];`
C) Both A and B
D) `str = "Hello"`

Answer: C) Both A and B

2. What function in MATLAB converts a string to uppercase?

A) `lower()`
B) `toupper()`
C) `upper()`
D) `capitalize()`

Answer: C) upper()

3. Which MATLAB function is used to concatenate strings?

A) `combine()`
B) `concat()`
C) `strcat()`
D) `concatenate()`

Answer: C) strcat()

4. How would you find the length of the string "MATLAB" in MATLAB?

A) `len("MATLAB")`
B) `length("MATLAB")`
C) `size("MATLAB")`
D) `numel("MATLAB")`

Answer: B) length("MATLAB")

5. What is the correct syntax for modifying a specific character in a character array?

A) `str(5) = 'X';`
B) `str[5] = 'X';`
C) `str[5] = "X";`
D) `str(5) = "X";`

Answer: A) str(5) = 'X';

6. What will the following MATLAB code return?

```
str = 'MATLAB';
result = upper(str);
```

A) `MATLAB`
B) `matlab`
C) `Matlab`
D) Error

Answer: A) MATLAB

---

7. Which of the following functions can be used to change a string to lowercase?

A) `lower()`
B) `tolower()`
C) `upper()`
D) `case()`

Answer: A) lower()

---

8. Which of the following MATLAB functions is used to replace part of a string with another string?

A) `replace()`
B) `substitute()`
C) `find()`
D) `modify()`

Answer: A) replace()

---

9. Which of the following is the correct syntax to concatenate two string arrays `str1` and `str2`?

A) `str1 + str2`
B) `str1 + ' ' + str2`
C) `concatenate(str1, str2)`
D) `strcat(str1, str2)`

Answer: D) strcat(str1, str2)

10. How would you modify the string `"Hello"` to replace `"e"` with `"a"`?

A) `replace("Hello", "e", "a")`
B) `str = replace("Hello", "e", "a")`
C) `Hello = replace(Hello, "e", "a")`
D) `str = "Hello".replace("e", "a")`

Answer: B) str = replace("Hello", "e", "a")

6.2 File Operations: Reading and Writing Text Files

11. Which of the following MATLAB functions is used to open a file for reading?

A) `open()`
B) `fopen('filename', 'r')`
C) `fopen('filename', 'w')`
D) `readfile('filename')`

Answer: B) fopen('filename', 'r')

---

12. Which of the following functions is used to close a file in MATLAB?

A) `close()`
B) `fclose()`
C) `end()`
D) `fend()`

Answer: B) fclose()

---

13. What does the `fread` function do in MATLAB?

A) It reads a string from a file.
B) It reads binary data from a file.
C) It writes text data to a file.
D) It writes binary data to a file.

Answer: B) It reads binary data from a file.

---

14. How do you write text to a file in MATLAB?

A) `fwrite()`
B) `fread()`
C) `fprintf()`
D) `write()`

Answer: C) fprintf()

---

15. Which file opening mode in `fopen` is used to create a new file for writing?

A) `'r'`
B) `'w'`
C) `'a'`
D) `'r+'`

Answer: B) 'w'

---

16. What will happen if you try to open a file with `fopen` using the mode `'r'` and the file doesn't exist?

A) It will create the file.
B) It will throw an error.
C) It will return an empty string.
D) It will return `-1`.

Answer: B) It will throw an error.

---

17. Which of the following MATLAB functions is used to write binary data to a file?

A) `fwrite()`
B) `fopen()`
C) `fprint()`
D) `writefile()`

Answer: A) fwrite()

18. What is the MATLAB command to open a file for appending data?

A) `fopen('file.txt', 'r')`
B) `fopen('file.txt', 'w')`
C) `fopen('file.txt', 'a')`
D) `fopen('file.txt', 'r+')`

Answer: C) fopen('file.txt', 'a')

---

19. How would you handle an error if a file cannot be opened using `fopen` in MATLAB?

A) `try-catch` block
B) `if(fid == -1)` check
C) `error()` function
D) All of the above

Answer: D) All of the above

---

20. What does `fclose()` do in MATLAB?

A) It writes data to a file.
B) It reads data from a file.
C) It closes an opened file.
D) It opens a file for reading.

Answer: C) It closes an opened file.

6.3 Sorting and Searching Text Data

21. What MATLAB function is used to sort an array in ascending order?

A) `sort()`
B) `arrange()`
C) `ascending()`
D) `order()`

Answer: A) sort()

---

22. How would you sort an array in descending order in MATLAB?

A) `sort(arr, 'descend')`
B) `sort(arr)`
C) `descend(arr)`
D) `reverse(arr)`

Answer: A) sort(arr, 'descend')

---

23. What is the purpose of the `linearSearch` function in MATLAB?

A) It sorts an array.
B) It finds the index of an element in an unsorted array.
C) It finds the median of an array.
D) It searches an element in a sorted array.

Answer: B) It finds the index of an element in an unsorted array.

---

24. What is the time complexity of a binary search algorithm?

A) O(n)
B) O(log n)
C) O(n^2)
D) O(n log n)

Answer: B) O(log n)

---

25. Which of the following is a requirement for using binary search in MATLAB?

A) The array must be sorted.
B) The array must contain only integers.
C) The array must have at least 10 elements.
D) The array must not contain duplicate values.

Answer: A) The array must be sorted.

6.1 String Handling in MATLAB

1. Write a MATLAB program to create a string "MATLAB" and print it to the console.

Answer:

```
str = "MATLAB";   % Create string
disp(str);   % Display the string
```

2. Write a function that converts a string input to uppercase.

Answer:

```
function upperStr = convertToUpper(str)
    upperStr = upper(str);   % Convert string to uppercase
end
```

Test:

```
result = convertToUpper('hello');
disp(result);   % Outputs: HELLO
```

3. Write a MATLAB program that takes a string as input and displays its length.

Answer:

```
str = input('Enter a string: ', 's');
len = length(str);   % Get the length of the string
disp(['Length of the string: ', num2str(len)]);
```

4. Write a MATLAB program to concatenate two strings, "Hello" and "World".

Answer:

```
str1 = "Hello";
str2 = "World";
result = str1 + " " + str2;   % Concatenate strings with space
disp(result);   % Outputs: Hello World
```

5. Write a function that replaces all occurrences of 'a' with 'o' in a given string.

Answer:

```
function modifiedStr = replaceAwithO(str)
    modifiedStr = replace(str, 'a', 'o');
end
```

Test:

```
result = replaceAwith0('banana');
disp(result);   % Outputs: bonono
```

6. Write a MATLAB program to convert a string "hello" to uppercase and then back to lowercase.

Answer:

```
str = 'hello';
upperStr = upper(str);   % Convert to uppercase
lowerStr = lower(upperStr);   % Convert back to lowercase
disp(lowerStr);   % Outputs: hello
```

7. Write a MATLAB function that checks if two strings are equal (case-sensitive).

Answer:

```
function isEqual = checkStringEquality(str1, str2)
    isEqual = strcmp(str1, str2);   % Compare strings
end
```

Test:

```
result = checkStringEquality('hello', 'hello');
disp(result);   % Outputs: 1 (true)
```

6.2 File Operations: Reading and Writing Text Files

8. Write a MATLAB program that opens a file named "data.txt" for reading and displays its content.

Answer:

```
fid = fopen('data.txt', 'r');   % Open the file for reading
if fid == -1
    error('File could not be opened');
end
content = fread(fid, '*char')';   % Read the content as characters
disp(content);   % Display the content
fclose(fid);   % Close the file
```

9. Write a MATLAB program that writes the string "Hello, World!" to a file called "output.txt".

Answer:

```
fid = fopen('output.txt', 'w');  % Open file for writing
if fid == -1
    error('File could not be opened');
end
fprintf(fid, 'Hello, World!\n');  % Write the string to the file
fclose(fid);  % Close the file
```

10. Write a function that reads the contents of a binary file and displays it.

Answer:

```
function readBinaryFile(filename)
    fid = fopen(filename, 'rb');  % Open file for reading binary data
    if fid == -1
        error('File could not be opened');
    end
    content = fread(fid, '*uint8');  % Read binary data as unsigned integers
    disp(content');  % Display the binary content
    fclose(fid);  % Close the file
end
```

11. Write a MATLAB program to append text to an existing file "log.txt".

Answer:

```
fid = fopen('log.txt', 'a');  % Open file for appending
if fid == -1
    error('File could not be opened');
end
fprintf(fid, 'New log entry\n');  % Append text to the file
fclose(fid);  % Close the file
```

12. Write a MATLAB function that reads a file "numbers.txt" containing integers, calculates their sum, and returns the result.

Answer:

```
function sumOfNumbers = sumNumbersFromFile(filename)
    fid = fopen(filename, 'r');  % Open the file for reading
    if fid == -1
        error('File could not be opened');
    end
    numbers = fscanf(fid, '%d');  % Read integers from the file
    sumOfNumbers = sum(numbers);  % Calculate the sum
    fclose(fid);  % Close the file
end
```

13. Write a MATLAB program that creates a new file "example.txt" and writes a list of names to it.

Answer:

```
fid = fopen('example.txt', 'w');  % Open the file for writing
if fid == -1
    error('File could not be opened');
end
names = {'Alice', 'Bob', 'Charlie'};
for i = 1:length(names)
    fprintf(fid, '%s\n', names{i});  % Write each name to the file
end
fclose(fid);  % Close the file
```

6.3 Sorting and Searching Text Data

14. Write a MATLAB function that sorts an array of strings alphabetically.

Answer:

```
function sortedArray = sortStrings(strArray)
    sortedArray = sort(strArray);  % Sort the string array alphabetically
end
```

Test:

```
sorted = sortStrings(["apple", "banana", "grape", "orange"]);
disp(sorted);  % Outputs: 'apple', 'banana', 'grape', 'orange'
```

15. Implement a binary search algorithm in MATLAB to find an element in a sorted array.

Answer:

```
function index = binarySearch(arr, target)
    left = 1;
    right = length(arr);
    while left <= right
        mid = floor((left + right) / 2);
        if arr(mid) == target
            index = mid;  % Target found
            return;
        elseif arr(mid) < target
            left = mid + 1;  % Search the right half
        else
            right = mid - 1;  % Search the left half
        end
    end
    index = -1;  % Target not found
end
```

Test:

```
arr = [1, 3, 5, 7, 9];
target = 5;
index = binarySearch(arr, target);
disp(index);  % Outputs: 3 (index of 5)
```

CHAPTER 7: CONTROL FLOW IN MATLAB

7.1 Conditional Statements in MATLAB

Conditional statements are a fundamental part of programming, allowing MATLAB programs to make decisions and execute specific blocks of code based on certain conditions. These conditions are typically logical expressions that evaluate to either true or false, directing the flow of execution based on those results. This makes conditional statements essential for handling different cases and controlling program behavior dynamically.

1. if, else, and elseif Statements

MATLAB provides three key statements—if, else, and elseif—to create conditional structures that control the flow of execution. Here's how each one works:

if Statement

The if statement is used to execute a block of code if a specific condition is true. If the condition evaluates to false, the code inside the if block is skipped.

Syntax:

```
if condition
    % Code to execute if condition is true
end
```

Example:

```
x = 5;
if x > 0
    disp('x is positive');
end
```

In this example, x is positive, so the message 'x is positive' will be displayed in the command window. If x were a negative number, the code inside the if block would be skipped.

else Statement

The else statement is paired with the if statement to execute a block of code when the condition in the if statement is false. You can think of it as a "default" action when none of the previous conditions are met.

Syntax:

```
if condition
    % Code if condition is true
else
    % Code if condition is false
```

```
end
```

Example:

```
x = -3;
if x > 0
    disp('x is positive');
else
    disp('x is not positive');
end
```

In this example, since x is negative, the message `'x is not positive'` will be displayed. The block inside the if is skipped because the condition x > 0 is false.

elseif Statement

The elseif statement allows you to check multiple conditions. If the condition in the if statement is false, MATLAB will evaluate the conditions in the elseif blocks. If none of the if or elseif conditions are true, the else block (if present) is executed.

Syntax:

```
if condition1
    % Code for condition1
elseif condition2
    % Code for condition2
else
    % Code if none of the above conditions are true
end
```

Example:

```
x = 0;
if x > 0
    disp('x is positive');
elseif x == 0
    disp('x is zero');
else
    disp('x is negative');
end
```

Here, x is 0, so the second condition (x == 0) evaluates to true, and the message `'x is zero'` is displayed.

2. Logical Expressions and Comparison Operators

Conditional statements often involve logical expressions and comparison operators, which allow you to compare variables and make decisions based on the results of these comparisons.

Comparison Operators

These operators are used to compare two values:

- ==: Equal to
- ~=: Not equal to
- >: Greater than
- <: Less than
- >=: Greater than or equal to
- <=: Less than or equal to

Example:

```
a = 5;
b = 10;
if a < b
    disp('a is less than b');
end
```

In this example, a is indeed less than b, so the message 'a is less than b' is displayed.

Logical Operators

Logical operators are used to combine multiple conditions in a more complex manner:

- &: Logical AND (both conditions must be true)
- |: Logical OR (either condition can be true)
- ~: Logical NOT (inverts the truth value)

Example using && (Logical AND) and || (Logical OR):

```
x = 5;
if x > 0 && x < 10
    disp('x is between 0 and 10');
end
```

Here, both conditions (x > 0 and x < 10) must be true for the code inside the if block to execute. Since x is 5, which satisfies both conditions, the message 'x is between 0 and 10' is displayed.

Example using || (Logical OR):

```
y = -3;
if y < 0 || y == 0
    disp('y is either negative or zero');
end
```

Here, only one condition needs to be true for the if block to execute. Since y is negative, the message 'y is either negative or zero' will be displayed.

Example using ~ (Logical NOT):

```
z = 10;
if ~(z == 0)
    disp('z is not zero');
end
```

In this case, the condition `z == 0` is false, so applying the logical NOT (~) makes it true, and the message `'z is not zero'` is displayed.

7.2 Repetition Statements in MATLAB

Repetition statements, also known as loops, are a fundamental part of programming. They allow certain blocks of code to be executed repeatedly until a condition is satisfied or for a specific number of times. In MATLAB, there are two primary types of loops: **while loops** and **for loops**. Additionally, MATLAB provides control statements like `break` and `continue` to control the flow of loops. Here's a detailed explanation of these concepts:

1. while Loop

A **while loop** in MATLAB allows you to repeat a block of code as long as a specified condition is true. The loop continues to execute the code inside it until the condition becomes false.

Syntax:

```
while condition
    % code to execute while the condition is true
end
```

- **condition**: This is a logical expression. The loop will keep executing the code as long as the condition evaluates to true.
- **code**: This is the block of code that gets executed repeatedly.

Example:

```
x = 1;
while x <= 5
    disp(x);          % Display the current value of x
    x = x + 1;        % Increment x by 1
end
```

In this example:

- The loop will continue as long as x <= 5.
- Initially, x is 1. The loop will display x, then increment x by 1.
- The loop will run five times, printing the values of x from 1 to 5.

- After x reaches 6, the condition x <= 5 becomes false, and the loop stops.

Output:

```
Copy
1
2
3
4
5
```

2. for Loop

A **for loop** in MATLAB is used to repeat a block of code for a specific number of times. It iterates over a range of values, typically from a start value to an end value.

Syntax:

```
for index = startValue:endValue
    % code to execute in each iteration
end
```

- **startValue**: The starting value of the loop.
- **endValue**: The end value. The loop will iterate over all values from startValue to endValue (inclusive).
- **index**: The loop variable that will take the value of each item in the range.

Example:

```
for i = 1:5
    disp(i);          % Display the current value of i
end
```

In this example:

- The loop starts with i = 1 and continues to i = 5.
- Each time the loop iterates, it displays the current value of i.

Output:

```
1
2
3
4
5
```

3. Loop Control with break and continue

MATLAB provides two important loop control statements: **break** and **continue**. These are used to change the flow of the loop under certain conditions.

break:

The break statement is used to exit a loop prematurely. When break is encountered inside a loop, the loop stops immediately, and control is passed to the next statement after the loop.

Example:

```
for i = 1:10
    if i == 6
        break;   % Exit loop when i is 6
    end
    disp(i);
end
```

In this example:

- The loop starts with i = 1 and continues until i = 6.
- When i equals 6, the break statement is executed, and the loop is terminated prematurely.

Output:

```
1
2
3
4
5
```

After printing 5, the loop is exited due to the break.

continue:

The continue statement is used to skip the current iteration of the loop and proceed to the next iteration. When continue is encountered, the remaining code in the current iteration is skipped, and the loop moves to the next value of the loop variable.

Example:

```
for i = 1:5
    if i == 3
        continue;   % Skip when i is 3
    end
    disp(i);
end
```

In this example:

- The loop runs through values of i from 1 to 5.

- When i equals 3, the `continue` statement is executed, which skips the `disp(i)` command for that iteration and proceeds to the next iteration.

Output:

```
1
2
4
5
```

As you can see, the value 3 is skipped in the output due to the `continue` statement.

7.3 Error Handling in MATLAB

Error handling is a crucial part of writing robust and reliable programs. In MATLAB, error handling is managed using the `try` and `catch` blocks. These blocks help you handle exceptions that may arise during code execution, allowing you to gracefully recover from errors rather than allowing the program to crash. Additionally, MATLAB provides several debugging tools to help identify and fix issues in your code.

---

1. Using `try` and `catch` for Error Management

The `try` and `catch` mechanism in MATLAB helps you manage errors by executing specific code when an error occurs.

`try` block:

- The `try` block contains the code that might produce an error. If an error occurs within the `try` block, MATLAB immediately transfers control to the corresponding `catch` block.
- If no error occurs in the `try` block, the `catch` block is skipped.

`catch` block:

- The `catch` block executes if an error occurs in the `try` block. You can use the `catch` block to handle errors, log the error, display custom error messages, or clean up resources.

Syntax:

```
try
    % Code that may cause an error
catch exception
    % Code to handle the error
    disp('Error occurred:');
    disp(exception.message);
```

```
end
```

- **exception**: The `catch` block can capture an exception object, which provides information about the error, such as the error message, the name of the error, and the stack trace.

Example:

```
try
    x = 5 / 0;  % This will cause a division by zero error
catch exception
    disp('An error occurred:');
    disp(exception.message);  % Display the error message
end
```

In this example:

- The code inside the `try` block attempts to divide 5 by 0, which causes a "division by zero" error.
- The `catch` block then captures the error and displays the error message: "An error occurred: Division by zero."

Output:

```
An error occurred:
Division by zero.
```

The `exception.message` contains the error message provided by MATLAB, which explains why the error occurred.

2. Debugging in MATLAB

MATLAB provides several tools to help with debugging, which allows you to inspect variables, control the flow of execution, and find errors in your code.

Breakpoints:

- **Breakpoints** are special points in the code where execution will pause, allowing you to inspect the current state of variables and step through the code line by line.
- You can set breakpoints in the MATLAB editor by clicking in the margin next to the line numbers. When the code reaches a breakpoint, execution halts, and MATLAB enters **debugging mode**.

Using `disp()` and `fprintf()`:

- **`disp()`** and **`fprintf()`** can be used to display the values of variables during code execution. These functions help track the program's state at different points in the execution flow.

`dbstop`:

- The **dbstop** command allows you to set breakpoints programmatically. For instance, you can set a breakpoint to stop the code when an error occurs, or you can stop at specific lines or functions.

Example:

```
% Set a breakpoint on the next line when an error occurs
dbstop if error

x = 10;
y = 0;
z = x / y;  % This will cause a division by zero error
```

In this example:

- The `dbstop if error` command tells MATLAB to stop execution when an error occurs, entering debugging mode.
- When the code executes and the error (x / y) is encountered, MATLAB will stop the program and enter **debugging mode**, allowing you to inspect the values of x, y, and z and investigate the cause of the error.

MATLAB Debugging Workflow:

1. **Set Breakpoints**: You can place breakpoints directly in the editor by clicking next to the line numbers or use `dbstop` to set breakpoints programmatically.
2. **Run the Code**: Execute your code normally. When the execution reaches a breakpoint or an error occurs, MATLAB will pause, and you can inspect the values of variables.
3. **Step Through the Code**: Use the debugging tools (Step In, Step Over, Step Out) to control the flow of execution and observe how variables change.
4. **Inspect Variables**: You can inspect the values of variables in the Workspace or use commands like `whos` and `disp()` to display variable values.
5. **Fix Errors**: Once you identify the cause of an error, you can fix the issue and continue running the code from the breakpoint.

Other Useful Debugging Commands:

- **dbstep**: Step through the code line by line.
- **dbup** and **dbdown**: Move up or down the call stack during debugging.
- **dbquit**: Exit debugging mode.

25 multiple-choice questions (MCQs):

7.1 Conditional Statements:

1. **Which of the following is the correct syntax for an `if` statement in MATLAB?**
   - o **A)** `if (condition) { code }`
   - o **B)** `if condition; code; end`
   - o **C)** `if condition code end`
   - o **D)** `if condition: code`

   Answer: B

2. **What will be the output of the following code?**

```
x = 10;
if x < 5
    disp('Less than 5');
elseif x == 10
    disp('Equal to 10');
else
    disp('Greater than 5');
end
```

   - o **A)** Less than 5
   - o **B)** Equal to 10
   - o **C)** Greater than 5
   - o **D)** No output

   Answer: B

3. **Which logical operator is used to check if two conditions are true in MATLAB?**
   - o **A)** &
   - o **B)** |
   - o **C)** !
   - o **D)** ==

   Answer: A

4. **In MATLAB, which of the following operators is used to check if two values are equal?**
   - o **A)** !=
   - o **B)** =
   - o **C)** ==
   - o **D)** =~

   Answer: C

5. **What does the following MATLAB code do?**

```
a = 5;
b = 10;
if a > b || b > 5
    disp('Condition met');
end
```

- o A) Displays "Condition met"
- o B) Does not display anything
- o C) Throws an error
- o D) Displays "b is greater than 5"

Answer: A

6. **Which of the following comparison operators is used to check if one value is greater than or equal to another in MATLAB?**
    - o A) >
    - o B) <
    - o C) >=
    - o D) ==

Answer: C

7. **Which of the following logical operators can be used to negate a condition in MATLAB?**
    - o A) ~
    - o B) &
    - o C) |
    - o D) ==

Answer: A

8. **What is the result of the following code?**

```
x = -2;
if x < 0
    disp('Negative');
elseif x == 0
    disp('Zero');
else
    disp('Positive');
end
```

- o A) Negative
- o B) Zero
- o C) Positive
- o D) No output

Answer: A

9. **In MATLAB, which of the following is the correct syntax for an `else` statement?**
   - o A) `else condition`
   - o B) `else if condition`
   - o C) `else`
   - o D) `if else condition`

   Answer: C

10. **Which of the following logical expressions would be true if `a` is 5 and `b` is 10 in MATLAB?**
    - o A) `a < b && b > 5`
    - o B) `a > b || b < 5`
    - o C) `a == b`
    - o D) `a != 5`

    Answer: A

7.2 Repetition Statements:

11. **What is the correct syntax for a `while` loop in MATLAB?**
    - o A) `while (condition) { code }`
    - o B) `while condition code end`
    - o C) `while condition { code }`
    - o D) `while condition code; end`

    Answer: D

12. **What will be the output of the following `while` loop?**

```
i = 1;
while i <= 3
    disp(i);
    i = i + 1;
end
```

   - o A) 1 2 3
   - o B) 0 1 2 3
   - o C) 1 1 1
   - o D) Error

   Answer: A

13. **Which of the following statements will make the loop skip the current iteration and proceed to the next?**
    - o A) `break`

B) `continue`
o C) `stop`
o D) `pause`

Answer: B

14. **What will the following `for` loop output?**

```
for i = 1:4
    disp(i);
end
```

     o A) 1 2 3
     o B) 1 2 3 4
     o C) 4 3 2 1
     o D) Error

Answer: B

15. **In MATLAB, which of the following is the correct syntax for a `for` loop?**
     o A) `for i = 1 to 5`
     o B) `for i = 1:5`
     o C) `for (i = 1, i <= 5)`
     o D) `for i to 5`

Answer: B

16. **What does the `break` statement do in a loop in MATLAB?**
     o A) Skips the current iteration and moves to the next
     o B) Exits the loop completely
     o C) Pauses the loop until further instructions
     o D) Stops the program entirely

Answer: B

17. **What will the following code display?**

```
for i = 1:5
    if i == 3
        continue;
    end
    disp(i);
end
```

     o A) 1 2 3 4 5
     o B) 1 2 4 5
     o C) 1 2 3
     o D) Error

Answer: B

18. **Which of the following is the correct way to define a loop that runs 10 times in MATLAB?**
    - o **A)** `for i = 10`
    - o **B)** `for i = 1 to 10`
    - o **C)** `for i = 1:10`
    - o **D)** `for 1:10`

    Answer: C

7.3 Error Handling:

19. **What is the purpose of the `try` block in MATLAB?**
    - o A) It handles errors that occur in the code.
    - o B) It contains code that might throw an error.
    - o C) It skips the error and continues execution.
    - o D) It sets breakpoints for debugging.

    Answer: B

20. **What will be displayed by the following code?**

```
try
    x = 1 / 0;   % Division by zero
catch exception
    disp('Error occurred');
    disp(exception.message);
end
```

    - o A) Error occurred
    - o B) Error: Division by zero
    - o C) An exception occurred
    - o D) Division by zero

    Answer: A

21. **Which of the following MATLAB commands is used to handle errors inside a `try` block?**
    - o **A)** `catch`
    - o **B)** `finally`
    - o **C)** `error`
    - o **D)** `return`

    Answer: A

22. **Which of the following MATLAB functions is used for debugging by allowing you to set a breakpoint?**
    - o A) `breakpoint()`
    - o B) `dbstop`
    - o C) `debugger()`
    - o D) `pause`

Answer: B

23. **What does the `dbstop if error` command do in MATLAB?**
    - o A) It sets a breakpoint on errors.
    - o B) It stops the program execution after a certain number of iterations.
    - o C) It stops the program if a specific condition is met.
    - o D) It triggers an error intentionally.

Answer: A

24. **Which of the following is the correct MATLAB syntax for the `catch` block?**
    - o A) `catch(exception)`
    - o B) `catch exception`
    - o C) `catch {exception}`
    - o D) `catch: exception`

Answer: B

25. **What does the `disp()` function do in MATLAB during debugging?**
    - o A) Displays error messages only
    - o B) Displays the values of variables during execution
    - o C) Sets breakpoints in the code
    - o D) Pauses the code execution

Answer: B

7.1 Conditional Statements

Q1: Write a program that checks if a number is positive, negative, or zero.

Answer:

```
x = input('Enter a number: ');
if x > 0
    disp('The number is positive');
elseif x < 0
    disp('The number is negative');
else
    disp('The number is zero');
end
```

Q2: Write a program that checks whether a given number is even or odd.

Answer:

```
x = input('Enter a number: ');
if mod(x, 2) == 0
    disp('The number is even');
else
    disp('The number is odd');
end
```

Q3: Write a program to find the largest of three numbers using `if`, `elseif`, and `else` statements.

Answer:

```
a = input('Enter first number: ');
b = input('Enter second number: ');
c = input('Enter third number: ');

if a > b && a > c
    disp('The largest number is:');
    disp(a);
elseif b > a && b > c
    disp('The largest number is:');
    disp(b);
else
    disp('The largest number is:');
    disp(c);
end
```

Q4: Write a program that uses logical operators to check if a number is between 10 and 20.

Answer:

```
x = input('Enter a number: ');
if x > 10 && x < 20
    disp('The number is between 10 and 20');
else
    disp('The number is not between 10 and 20');
end
```

Q5: Write a program that checks if a number is divisible by both 3 and 5.

Answer:

```
x = input('Enter a number: ');
if mod(x, 3) == 0 && mod(x, 5) == 0
```

```
    disp('The number is divisible by both 3 and 5');
else
    disp('The number is not divisible by both 3 and 5');
end
```

7.2 Repetition Statements

Q6: Write a program that prints numbers from 1 to 10 using a for loop.

Answer:

```
for i = 1:10
    disp(i);
end
```

Q7: Write a program to calculate the sum of the first 100 integers using a while loop.

Answer:

```
i = 1;
sum = 0;
while i <= 100
    sum = sum + i;
    i = i + 1;
end
disp('The sum of the first 100 integers is:');
disp(sum);
```

Q8: Write a program that prints all even numbers between 1 and 20 using a for loop.

Answer:

```
for i = 2:2:20
    disp(i);
end
```

Q9: Write a program that finds the factorial of a number using a while loop.

Answer:

```
n = input('Enter a number: ');
fact = 1;
i = 1;
while i <= n
    fact = fact * i;
    i = i + 1;
```

```
end
disp('The factorial is:');
disp(fact);
```

Q10: Write a program that uses the `continue` statement to skip printing multiples of 3 in a range from 1 to 15.

Answer:

```
for i = 1:15
    if mod(i, 3) == 0
        continue;  % Skip multiples of 3
    end
    disp(i);
end
```

Q11: Write a program that uses the `break` statement to stop a loop when a number greater than 10 is encountered.

Answer:

```
for i = 1:20
    if i > 10
        break;  % Stop the loop when i is greater than 10
    end
    disp(i);
end
```

7.3 Error Handling

Q12: Write a program that divides two numbers but catches any error that might occur (e.g., division by zero) using `try` and `catch`.

Answer:

```
try
    a = input('Enter numerator: ');
    b = input('Enter denominator: ');
    result = a / b;
    disp('The result is:');
    disp(result);
catch exception
    disp('An error occurred:');
    disp(exception.message);
end
```

Q13: Write a program that attempts to read a file but catches any error if the file does not exist.

Answer:

```
try
    fid = fopen('nonexistent_file.txt', 'r');
    if fid == -1
        error('File not found');
    end
    data = fread(fid, '*char');
    disp('File contents:');
    disp(data);
    fclose(fid);
catch exception
    disp('Error occurred:');
    disp(exception.message);
end
```

Q14: Write a program that handles division by zero using `try` and `catch`. The program should display a custom message if an error occurs.

Answer:

```
try
    num = input('Enter numerator: ');
    denom = input('Enter denominator: ');
    result = num / denom;
    disp('The result is:');
    disp(result);
catch
    disp('Cannot divide by zero. Please enter a valid denominator.');
end
```

Q15: Write a program that causes an error intentionally (e.g., divide by zero) and uses `dbstop` to set a breakpoint when an error occurs.

Answer:

```
dbstop if error  % Set a breakpoint for any error
x = 5;
y = 0;
z = x / y;  % This will cause a division by zero error
```

- This code will stop execution at the point of error, allowing you to inspect the variables x, y, and z.

CHAPTER 8: DATA HANDLING AND FILE OPERATIONS

8.1 Writing and Reading Data Files in MATLAB

In MATLAB, working with data files is crucial for managing and storing information that can be used for further processing or analysis. MATLAB provides a variety of functions to handle different types of data files, including text files, binary files, CSV files, and MAT files. These file handling operations are essential for data persistence and for interfacing with external data sources.

Handling Text and Binary Files in MATLAB

1. Text Files

Text files store data as human-readable characters. These are often used for saving logs, configuration data, or other simple text-based data.

Opening a File

To read from or write to a file in MATLAB, the `fopen` function is used. It opens the file and returns a file identifier (`fid`) that is used in subsequent operations. When you're done, you must close the file using `fclose`.

- **Syntax**:

```
fid = fopen('filename', 'mode');
```

  o `'r'`: Open for reading.
  o `'w'`: Open for writing (creates or overwrites the file).
  o `'a'`: Open for appending (writes to the end of the file).
  o `'r+'`: Open for both reading and writing.
- **Example**:

```
fid = fopen('data.txt', 'w');  % Open for writing (create or overwrite
the file)
if fid == -1
    error('File could not be opened');
end
```

Reading from a Text File

To read data from a text file, you can use several functions such as `fgets`, `fscanf`, or `fread`. `fgets` is typically used for reading one line at a time.

- **Example**:

```
fid = fopen('data.txt', 'r');  % Open for reading
line = fgets(fid);  % Reads one line from the file
disp(line);
fclose(fid);  % Don't forget to close the file!
```

Writing to a Text File

To write to a file, you can use the `fprintf` function, which allows you to format the output data.

- **Example**:

```
fid = fopen('data.txt', 'w');  % Open file for writing
fprintf(fid, 'This is a test data line.\n');  % Write formatted text
fclose(fid);  % Close the file
```

2. Binary Files

Binary files store data in a non-human-readable format. This format is typically used for storing large datasets or data that requires efficient processing. Binary files are generally smaller and faster to read/write compared to text files.

Writing to a Binary File

Use the `fwrite` function to write binary data to a file. You can specify the data type (e.g., `int32`, `float64`) for the data being written.

- **Example**:

```
fid = fopen('data.bin', 'w');  % Open binary file for writing
fwrite(fid, [1, 2, 3, 4, 5], 'int32');  % Write 32-bit integers to the
file
fclose(fid);  % Close the file
```

Reading from a Binary File

Use `fread` to read binary data from a file. You should specify the format of the data being read (e.g., `'int32'` for 32-bit integers).

- **Example**:

```
fid = fopen('data.bin', 'r');  % Open binary file for reading
data = fread(fid, 'int32');  % Read 32-bit integers from the file
fclose(fid);  % Close the file
disp(data);  % Display the data
```

Working with CSV and MAT Files

1. CSV Files (Comma-Separated Values)

CSV files store data in tabular format, with rows separated by line breaks and columns separated by commas. These files are commonly used for exchanging data between different programs (e.g., Excel, databases).

Writing to a CSV File

MATLAB has several functions for reading and writing CSV files, including `csvwrite`, `writetable`, and `writecell`. The `csvwrite` function writes numeric data to a CSV file.

- **Example:**

```
data = [1, 2, 3; 4, 5, 6];  % Example data
csvwrite('data.csv', data);  % Write data to a CSV file
```

Reading from a CSV File

The `csvread` function is used to read numeric data from a CSV file. If the file contains non-numeric data or headers, `readtable` is a better choice.

- **Example:**

```
data = csvread('data.csv');  % Read numeric data from CSV
disp(data);  % Display the data
```

Using `readtable` and `writetable`

For CSV files with mixed data types (e.g., numbers and text) or headers, `readtable` and `writetable` are recommended. These functions read and write data as tables, which are more flexible and easier to work with.

- **Example:**

```
T = readtable('data.csv');  % Read data from a CSV file into a table
disp(T);  % Display the table
writetable(T, 'output.csv');  % Write the table to a new CSV file
```

2. MAT Files

MAT files are MATLAB's native format for saving variables. They allow you to store variables in a binary format, preserving their types, sizes, and values. This format is ideal for saving and sharing MATLAB workspaces or large data structures.

Saving Variables to a MAT File

Use the `save` function to save variables to a MAT file. You can save one or multiple variables at once.

- **Example**:

```
A = rand(3, 3);   % Example matrix
B = [1, 2, 3];    % Example vector
save('data.mat', 'A', 'B');  % Save variables A and B to the MAT file
```

Loading Variables from a MAT File

Use the `load` function to load variables from a MAT file into the MATLAB workspace. All variables saved in the MAT file will be loaded by default unless specified otherwise.

- **Example**:

```
load('data.mat');  % Load all variables from the MAT file
disp(A);  % Display variable A
disp(B);  % Display variable B
```

Summary of File Handling Functions

File Type	Function	Purpose
Text Files	`fopen, fclose, fgets, fprintf, fscanf`	Open/close files, read/write text data
Binary Files	`fopen, fclose, fwrite, fread`	Open/close files, read/write binary data
CSV Files	`csvwrite, csvread, writetable, readtable`	Write/read numeric data or tables in CSV format
MAT Files	`save, load`	Save/load variables in MATLAB's native .mat format

8.2 Sorting and Randomizing Lists

MATLAB provides a variety of built-in functions that make working with arrays and lists easy, especially when you need to sort or randomize them. This section explains how you can use MATLAB's sorting and randomizing functions and even implement your own sorting algorithms.

1. Sorting Arrays

The `sort` function in MATLAB is commonly used to arrange elements in either ascending or descending order. Here are the basic usages:

a. Sorting a vector in ascending order:

The default behavior of the `sort` function is to sort in ascending order.

- Example:

```
A = [5, 2, 8, 1];
B = sort(A);  % Sorts A in ascending order
disp(B);  % Outputs [1, 2, 5, 8]
```

In this example, the array `A` is sorted from smallest to largest value, and the result is stored in `B`.

b. Sorting a vector in descending order:

You can specify that you want to sort in descending order by passing the string `'descend'` as an argument.

- Example:

```
B = sort(A, 'descend');  % Sorts A in descending order
disp(B);  % Outputs [8, 5, 2, 1]
```

In this case, the array `A` is sorted from largest to smallest value.

c. Sorting matrices:

When sorting matrices, `sort` works by default on each column. It sorts each column independently in ascending order.

- Example:

```
M = [3, 2, 1; 9, 7, 5];
sortedM = sort(M);  % Sorts each column
disp(sortedM);
```

Output:

```
sortedM =
     3     2     1
     9     7     5
```

In this case, each column is sorted independently, but no rows are sorted.

2. Randomizing Arrays

In addition to sorting, you can randomize arrays in MATLAB. This is often useful when you need to shuffle the order of elements in an array or generate random permutations.

a. Random permutation of integers:

The `randperm` function generates a random permutation of integers. This can be useful to shuffle the order of indices or create random orderings.

- Example:

```
n = 5;
randomPermutation = randperm(n);   % Random permutation of integers 1 to 5
disp(randomPermutation);
```

This will output a random permutation of the integers from 1 to 5. For example:

```
randomPermutation =
     3     1     4     5     2
```

The output can vary each time you run it, as the permutation is random.

b. Shuffling an array:

You can use `randperm` to shuffle the elements of an existing array. By using the length of the array as an argument for `randperm`, you can obtain a randomized index array, and then apply that index to shuffle the original array.

- Example:

```
A = [1, 2, 3, 4, 5];
shuffledA = A(randperm(length(A)));   % Shuffle the array
disp(shuffledA);
```

This will output a randomly shuffled version of the array `A`, such as:

```
shuffledA =
     4     2     5     1     3
```

Implementing Sorting Algorithms

Although MATLAB provides highly optimized built-in sorting functions, it can also be valuable to understand how sorting algorithms work under the hood. One common algorithm for sorting is **Bubble Sort**.

Bubble Sort Algorithm:

The Bubble Sort algorithm compares adjacent elements in the array and swaps them if they are in the wrong order. This process is repeated until the entire array is sorted.

- Example of the **Bubble Sort** implementation:

```
function sortedArray = bubbleSort(A)
    n = length(A);  % Get the number of elements in A
    for i = 1:n-1  % Iterate through all elements
        for j = 1:n-i  % Iterate through the remaining elements
            if A(j) > A(j+1)  % Compare adjacent elements
                % Swap if elements are in the wrong order
                temp = A(j);
                A(j) = A(j+1);
                A(j+1) = temp;
            end
        end
    end
    sortedArray = A;  % Return the sorted array
end
```

In the `bubbleSort` function:

- The outer loop ensures that we repeat the sorting process for all elements.
- The inner loop compares adjacent elements, and if the left element is larger than the right, it swaps them.
- This continues until no more swaps are needed, meaning the array is sorted.
- Example usage:

```
A = [5, 2, 8, 1];
sortedA = bubbleSort(A);
disp(sortedA);  % Output will be [1, 2, 5, 8]
```

8.3 Searching Data in MATLAB

Searching for data within arrays or lists is a fundamental operation in many programming tasks. MATLAB provides multiple ways to search for data using both manual methods (like linear and binary search) and built-in functions that are highly optimized. Let's go over the various searching techniques in detail.

1. Linear Search

Linear search is a simple method of searching for an element in an array or list. It checks each element, one by one, from the beginning until it finds the target element. This approach is effective for unsorted lists but can be inefficient for large datasets since it checks every element.

- **How it works:**
    1. Start from the first element of the array.
    2. Compare each element with the target.

3. If a match is found, return the index of that element.
4. If no match is found by the end of the list, return -1 (indicating that the element does not exist in the array).

- **MATLAB Implementation:**

```
function index = linearSearch(arr, target)
    index = -1;  % Default value if target is not found
    for i = 1:length(arr)
        if arr(i) == target
            index = i;  % Return the index if target is found
            break;  % Exit the loop once the target is found
        end
    end
end
```

- **Example usage:**

```
arr = [10, 20, 30, 40, 50];
target = 30;
idx = linearSearch(arr, target);  % Returns 3 (index of 30)
disp(idx);  % Output: 3
```

In this example, `linearSearch` checks each element of `arr` until it finds `30`, which is located at index 3.

---

2. Binary Search

Binary search is a more efficient search algorithm compared to linear search, but it requires the array to be sorted. It works by repeatedly dividing the search interval in half. If the target is smaller than the middle element, the search continues in the left half; if the target is greater, the search continues in the right half.

- **How it works:**
    1. Start by sorting the array (if it's not already sorted).
    2. Compare the middle element with the target.
    3. If the target is equal to the middle element, return the index.
    4. If the target is less than the middle element, continue searching the left half.
    5. If the target is greater than the middle element, continue searching the right half.
    6. If no match is found, return -1 (indicating that the target is not present).
- **MATLAB Implementation:**

```
function index = binarySearch(arr, target)
    arr = sort(arr);  % Ensure the array is sorted before searching
    left = 1;
    right = length(arr);

    while left <= right
        mid = floor((left + right) / 2);  % Find the middle index
```

```
        if arr(mid) == target
            index = mid;  % Return the index if the target is found
            return;
        elseif arr(mid) < target
            left = mid + 1;  % Continue search in the right half
        else
            right = mid - 1;  % Continue search in the left half
        end
    end

    index = -1;  % Return -1 if target is not found
end
```

- **Example usage:**

```
arr = [10, 20, 30, 40, 50];
target = 30;
idx = binarySearch(arr, target);  % Returns 3 (index of 30)
disp(idx);  % Output: 3
```

In this case, the array is sorted before the binary search begins. The search finds the target 30 at index 3.

3. MATLAB Built-in Functions for Searching

MATLAB provides several built-in functions for searching, which are optimized for performance and ease of use. Below are some of the commonly used functions for searching data in MATLAB.

- **find function:** The find function returns the indices of elements in an array that satisfy a given condition. It is useful when you want to find all occurrences of a particular value or condition in an array.
  - **Syntax:**

  ```
  idx = find(condition)
  ```

  - **Example usage:**

  ```
  A = [10, 20, 30, 40];
  idx = find(A == 30);  % Find the index where A equals 30
  disp(idx);  % Output: 3
  ```

  In this example, find(A == 30) returns the index where the value 30 is found in the array A.

- **ismember function:** The ismember function checks if elements of one array are present in another array. It returns a logical array where 1 represents true (if the element is present) and 0 represents false (if the element is absent).

     o **Syntax:**

```
result = ismember(A, B)
```

     o **Example usage:**

```
A = [10, 20, 30];
B = [20, 40, 60];
result = ismember(A, B);  % Checks which elements of A are in B
disp(result);  % Output: [0 1 0]
```

In this example, the function checks if the elements of A are present in B. The output [0 1 0] indicates that only the value 20 from A is present in B.

25 multiple-choice questions (MCQs)

8.1 Writing and Reading Data Files

1. Which of the following functions in MATLAB is used to open a file for writing?

a) fread
b) fopen
c) fclose
d) fwrite

Answer: b) fopen

---

2. Which file mode in MATLAB opens a file for both reading and writing?

a) 'r'
b) 'w'
c) 'r+'
d) 'a'

Answer: c) 'r+'

---

3. Which function would you use to write data to a binary file in MATLAB?

a) fscanf
b) fwrite

c) `fprintf`
d) `fgets`

Answer: b) `fwrite`

---

4. How do you read a single line from a text file in MATLAB?

a) `fgetl`
b) `fread`
c) `fgets`
d) `fscanf`

Answer: c) `fgets`

---

5. What function in MATLAB is used to read numeric data from a CSV file?

a) `readtable`
b) `csvread`
c) `fscanf`
d) `load`

Answer: b) `csvread`

---

6. Which of the following functions is used to save variables in a MAT file in MATLAB?

a) `write`
b) `load`
c) `save`
d) `saveas`

Answer: c) `save`

---

7. To load data from a MAT file into MATLAB, you would use which function?

a) `load`
b) `import`
c) `fscanf`
d) `readmat`

Answer: a) `load`

---

8. What is the purpose of the `fclose` function in MATLAB?

a) Closes the active MATLAB session
b) Closes the file after reading or writing
c) Opens a new file for reading
d) Erases the content of the file

Answer: b) Closes the file after reading or writing

---

9. Which of the following MATLAB functions is used for writing data in CSV format with more complex data structures like tables?

a) `csvwrite`
b) `writecsv`
c) `readtable`
d) `writetable`

Answer: d) `writetable`

---

10. In MATLAB, which command opens a file in append mode?

a) 'a'
b) 'w'
c) 'r+'
d) 'w+'

Answer: a) 'a'

8.2 Sorting and Randomizing Lists

11. What function is used to sort a matrix in MATLAB?

a) `sortrows`
b) `sort`
c) `organize`
d) `arrange`

Answer: b) `sort`

---

12. By default, which order does the `sort` function use to sort data in MATLAB?

a) Descending
b) Ascending
c) Random
d) It asks the user for preference

Answer: b) Ascending

---

13. If you want to sort an array in descending order in MATLAB, which command would you use?

a) `sort(A, 'descend')`
b) `sort(A, 'ascending')`
c) `sortdesc(A)`
d) `descendsort(A)`

Answer: a) `sort(A, 'descend')`

---

14. In MATLAB, which function would you use to randomize or shuffle the elements of an array?

a) `randshuffle`
b) `shuffle`
c) `randperm`
d) `rand`

Answer: c) `randperm`

---

15. Which MATLAB function would you use to sort the rows of a matrix based on the elements in each row?

a) `sort`
b) `sortrows`
c) `sortmatrix`
d) `matrixsort`

Answer: b) `sortrows`

---

16. Which sorting algorithm does MATLAB's `sort` function typically use?

a) Quick Sort
b) Bubble Sort
c) Merge Sort
d) MATLAB uses multiple algorithms and selects the most efficient one based on the data size and type.

Answer: d) MATLAB uses multiple algorithms and selects the most efficient one based on the data size and type.

---

17. Which of the following sorting algorithms involves repeatedly swapping adjacent elements to sort an array?

a) Quick Sort
b) Insertion Sort
c) Bubble Sort
d) Merge Sort

Answer: c) Bubble Sort

---

18. In MATLAB, what does the `randperm(n)` function return?

a) A random number between 0 and n
b) A matrix of random numbers
c) A random permutation of the integers from 1 to n
d) A sorted array of the first n integers

Answer: c) A random permutation of the integers from 1 to n

---

19. What does the function `randperm` generate when applied to an array A?

a) A random matrix
b) A random index set to reorder the array
c) A permutation of A
d) A sorted version of the array

Answer: b) A random index set to reorder the array

---

20. In MATLAB, what does the `randperm` function accept as its argument?

a) Any array
b) A scalar integer n
c) A cell array
d) A character string

Answer: b) A scalar integer n

8.3 Searching Data in MATLAB

21. Which of the following is the basic concept of linear search?

a) Repeatedly divides the array into two parts
b) Compares each element one by one to find the target
c) Sorts the array before searching
d) It searches in sorted order only

Answer: b) Compares each element one by one to find the target

---

22. Which MATLAB function is used to perform a binary search?

a) `binarySearch`
b) `find`
c) `ismember`
d) MATLAB does not have a built-in binary search function

Answer: d) MATLAB does not have a built-in binary search function

---

23. What condition must be met for binary search to work efficiently in MATLAB?

a) The list must be sorted
b) The array must be of even length
c) The list must contain unique elements
d) The array must be sorted in descending order

Answer: a) The list must be sorted

---

24. Which MATLAB function can be used to find the indices of elements in an array that satisfy a certain condition?

a) `find`
b) `locate`
c) `index`
d) `search`

Answer: a) `find`

---

25. What does the MATLAB function `ismember` do?

a) Checks if two arrays are identical
b) Finds the index of the element in an array
c) Checks if elements of one array are present in another
d) Sorts an array

Answer: c) Checks if elements of one array are present in another

8.1 Writing and Reading Data Files

1. Question:

Write a MATLAB program that creates a text file called `data.txt`, writes the string "Hello, World!" into it, and then closes the file.

Answer:

```
fid = fopen('data.txt', 'w');  % Open file for writing
fprintf(fid, 'Hello, World!\n');  % Write to the file
fclose(fid);  % Close the file
```

---

2. Question:

Write a MATLAB program that reads the content of the `data.txt` file (created in the previous question) and displays it.

Answer:

```
fid = fopen('data.txt', 'r');  % Open file for reading
```

```
content = fgets(fid);   % Read the content
disp(content);   % Display the content
fclose(fid);   % Close the file
```

3. Question:

Create a binary file `data.bin` that stores an array of integers `[1, 2, 3, 4, 5]` in MATLAB and then read the data back from the file.

Answer:

```
% Writing to binary file
fid = fopen('data.bin', 'w');
fwrite(fid, [1, 2, 3, 4, 5], 'int32');
fclose(fid);

% Reading from binary file
fid = fopen('data.bin', 'r');
data = fread(fid, 'int32');
disp(data);
fclose(fid);
```

4. Question:

Write a MATLAB program to save a matrix `A = [1, 2; 3, 4]` to a MAT file called `matrix_data.mat` and load it back.

Answer:

```
A = [1, 2; 3, 4];
save('matrix_data.mat', 'A');   % Save matrix to MAT file

% Load the matrix from the MAT file
load('matrix_data.mat');
disp(A);
```

5. Question:

Write a MATLAB program that reads a CSV file `data.csv`, which contains numeric data, and displays the contents as a matrix.

Answer:

```
data = csvread('data.csv');
disp(data);
```

6. Question:

Write a MATLAB program that writes a table of data to a CSV file `output.csv` using the `writetable` function.

Answer:

```
T = table([1; 2; 3], [4; 5; 6], 'VariableNames', {'A', 'B'});
writetable(T, 'output.csv');  % Write table to CSV file
```

8.2 Sorting and Randomizing Lists

7. Question:

Write a MATLAB program to sort the array `A = [3, 1, 4, 1, 5, 9, 2, 6]` in ascending order.

Answer:

```
A = [3, 1, 4, 1, 5, 9, 2, 6];
sortedA = sort(A);  % Sort in ascending order
disp(sortedA);
```

8. Question:

Write a MATLAB program to sort the matrix `M = [3, 2, 1; 6, 5, 4]` by columns in ascending order.

Answer:

```
M = [3, 2, 1; 6, 5, 4];
sortedM = sort(M);  % Sort each column in ascending order
disp(sortedM);
```

9. Question:

Write a MATLAB program to shuffle the elements of the array `A = [1, 2, 3, 4, 5]` randomly.

Answer:

```
A = [1, 2, 3, 4, 5];
shuffledA = A(randperm(length(A)));  % Shuffle the array
disp(shuffledA);
```

10. Question:

Write a MATLAB function that implements the bubble sort algorithm to sort an array `A` in ascending order.

Answer:

```
function sortedArray = bubbleSort(A)
    n = length(A);
    for i = 1:n-1
        for j = 1:n-i
            if A(j) > A(j+1)
                temp = A(j);
                A(j) = A(j+1);
                A(j+1) = temp;
            end
        end
    end
    sortedArray = A;   % Return the sorted array
end
```

11. Question:
Write a MATLAB program to sort the array `A = [10, 20, 5, 30, 25]` in descending order.
Answer:
```
A = [10, 20, 5, 30, 25];
sortedA = sort(A, 'descend');   % Sort in descending order
disp(sortedA);
```

8.3 Searching Data in MATLAB

12. Question:

Write a MATLAB function to perform a linear search on an array `arr` to find the index of a target value.

Answer:

```
function index = linearSearch(arr, target)
    index = -1;   % Return -1 if target is not found
    for i = 1:length(arr)
        if arr(i) == target
            index = i;   % Return the index if found
            break;
        end
    end
end
```

13. Question:

Write a MATLAB program to use the linear search function to find the index of the value 50 in the array `arr = [10, 20, 30, 40, 50]`.

Answer:

```
arr = [10, 20, 30, 40, 50];
target = 50;
idx = linearSearch(arr, target);   % Returns 5 (index of 50)
disp(idx);
```

14. Question:

Write a MATLAB function that implements the binary search algorithm on a sorted array `arr` to find the index of a target value.

Answer:

```
function index = binarySearch(arr, target)
    left = 1;
    right = length(arr);
    while left <= right
        mid = floor((left + right) / 2);
        if arr(mid) == target
            index = mid;
            return;
        elseif arr(mid) < target
            left = mid + 1;
        else
            right = mid - 1;
        end
    end
    index = -1;   % Target not found
end
```

15. Question:

Write a MATLAB program to use binary search to find the index of the value 30 in the sorted array `arr = [10, 20, 30, 40, 50]`.

Answer:

```
arr = [10, 20, 30, 40, 50];
target = 30;
idx = binarySearch(arr, target);   % Returns 3 (index of 30)
disp(idx);
```

CHAPTER 9: ADVANCED TOPICS IN MATLAB PROGRAMMING

9.1 MATLAB Functions for Data Analysis

MATLAB is a powerful environment specifically designed for numerical computing, and it is widely used for a variety of data analysis tasks. It provides a vast range of built-in functions for handling matrices, performing linear algebra operations, solving systems of equations, and applying numerical methods like integration, differentiation, and interpolation. Below, we'll discuss the key aspects of MATLAB's capabilities for data analysis, focusing on matrix manipulations, eigenvalues, linear algebra, and various numerical methods.

---

1. Matrix Manipulations, Eigenvalues, and Linear Algebra

MATLAB is fundamentally built around matrix operations, making it a strong tool for linear algebra tasks. It offers various functions to manipulate matrices, calculate eigenvalues, eigenvectors, and solve systems of linear equations.

Matrix Manipulations:

MATLAB allows you to easily create, manipulate, and perform operations on matrices. Below are common operations:

- **Matrix Creation**:
  - You can create matrices directly using arrays or built-in functions. For example:

    ```
    A = [1, 2; 3, 4];  % A 2x2 matrix
    B = magic(3);  % 3x3 magic square matrix (a square matrix where
    the sums of rows, columns, and diagonals are equal)
    ```

- **Matrix Addition and Subtraction**:
  - You can perform matrix addition and subtraction by simply using the + and – operators. Both matrices must have the same dimensions.

    ```
    C = A + B;  % Adds matrix A and matrix B
    D = A - B;  % Subtracts matrix B from matrix A
    ```

- **Matrix Multiplication**:
  - To multiply matrices, use the * operator. This operation is performed if the number of columns in the first matrix equals the number of rows in the second matrix.

    ```
    E = A * B;  % Matrix multiplication of A and B
    ```

- **Transposing a Matrix**:
  - The transpose of a matrix flips its rows and columns. In MATLAB, you can obtain the transpose by using the . ' operator.

```
AT = A.';   % Transpose of matrix A
```

Eigenvalues and Eigenvectors:

Eigenvalues and eigenvectors are crucial in many linear algebra applications, especially in systems of differential equations, stability analysis, and more. MATLAB provides the `eig` function to compute the eigenvalues and eigenvectors of a matrix.

- **Computing Eigenvalues and Eigenvectors**: The `eig` function returns the eigenvalues in a diagonal matrix and the eigenvectors as the columns of a matrix.

```
A = [4, -2; 1, 1];   % Example matrix
[eigenvectors, eigenvalues] = eig(A);   % Compute eigenvectors and
eigenvalues
disp('Eigenvalues:');
disp(diag(eigenvalues));   % Display eigenvalues
disp('Eigenvectors:');
disp(eigenvectors);   % Display eigenvectors
```

In this example, `eig(A)` calculates the eigenvalues and eigenvectors of matrix `A`. The eigenvalues are stored in a diagonal matrix, and the eigenvectors are stored in a matrix with each column representing an eigenvector.

Solving Linear Systems:

In many applications, you need to solve systems of linear equations of the form $A \cdot x = b$, where `A` is a matrix, `x` is a vector of unknowns, and `b` is a vector of constants. MATLAB provides an efficient way to solve this using the backslash operator `\`.

- **Solving a Linear System**:

```
A = [3, 2; 1, 4];   % Coefficient matrix
b = [5; 6];          % Right-hand side vector
x = A\b;             % Solve the system Ax = b
disp(x);             % Display the solution
```

The backslash operator `\` in MATLAB efficiently solves the system of equations by internally choosing the best algorithm (LU decomposition, for example).

---

2. Built-in MATLAB Functions for Numerical Methods

MATLAB provides a rich set of built-in functions to perform various numerical methods. These functions are used in data analysis tasks such as numerical integration, differentiation, and interpolation. Below are some important functions for these tasks:

Numerical Integration:

Numerical integration refers to approximating the integral of a function when an exact solution is difficult or impossible to obtain. MATLAB provides several functions to perform numerical integration.

- **Using the `integral` Function**: The `integral` function is used for performing numerical integration of functions over a specified interval.

```
f = @(x) x.^2;  % Define the function f(x) = x^2
integral_value = integral(f, 0, 1);  % Integrate f(x) from 0 to 1
disp(integral_value);  % Display the result
```

In this example, MATLAB calculates the integral of $x2x^2x2$ over the interval $[0, 1]$ using an adaptive quadrature method.

- **Using the `trapz` Function**: The `trapz` function performs numerical integration using the trapezoidal rule.

```
x = 0:0.1:10;  % Define x values
y = sin(x);    % Define the function y = sin(x)
integral_value = trapz(x, y);  % Numerical integration using
trapezoidal rule
disp(integral_value);  % Display the result
```

Differentiation:

Numerical differentiation is the process of approximating the derivative of a function. MATLAB provides the `diff` function, which computes the difference between consecutive elements of an array.

- **Using the `diff` Function**:

```
f = @(x) x.^2;  % Define the function f(x) = x^2
x = linspace(0, 10, 100);  % Generate 100 equally spaced points from 0
to 10
y = f(x);  % Calculate function values at each x point
dy = diff(y) ./ diff(x);  % Numerical derivative using the difference
quotient
```

In this example, we calculate the derivative of $x2x^2x2$ by taking the difference between consecutive values of y and dividing by the difference between consecutive values of x.

Interpolation:

Interpolation is the process of estimating unknown values between known data points. MATLAB provides various functions for interpolation, including `interp1` for 1D interpolation.

- **Using the `interp1` Function**:

```
x = [1, 2, 3, 4];  % Known x values
```

```
y = [2, 4, 6, 8];  % Known y values
y_interp = interp1(x, y, 2.5);  % Interpolate at x = 2.5
disp(y_interp);  % Display the interpolated value
```

The function `interp1` interpolates the value at x=2.5x = 2.5x=2.5 based on the known data points `x` and `y`.

9.2 Using External Libraries and Toolboxes

MATLAB is a versatile platform for numerical computing and data analysis. One of its strengths is the ability to expand its functionality through external libraries and specialized toolboxes. These toolboxes provide functions for a wide range of applications, from signal processing to machine learning, optimization, and image processing. In addition, MATLAB can integrate with low-level programming languages like C to leverage high-performance libraries. Let's explore these aspects in more detail.

---

1. Exploring MATLAB Toolboxes (Statistics, Signal Processing, etc.)

MATLAB toolboxes are collections of specialized functions that extend the base MATLAB environment. These toolboxes are designed to handle specific tasks or domains, making it easier for users to work in those areas without reinventing the wheel.

Common MATLAB Toolboxes:

1. **Statistics and Machine Learning Toolbox**: This toolbox provides a wide range of functions for statistical analysis, hypothesis testing, regression, classification, clustering, and more. It is an essential toolkit for anyone working in data analysis or predictive modeling.

   Example: **Linear Regression with `fitlm`** The `fitlm` function fits a linear regression model to a set of data. Here's how you can use it to model a simple linear relationship between `X` and `Y`:

   ```
   X = [1; 2; 3; 4; 5];  % Input data (predictors)
   Y = [2; 4; 6; 8; 10]; % Output data (responses)
   mdl = fitlm(X, Y);  % Fit linear regression model
   disp(mdl);  % Display model results
   ```

   This creates a linear regression model, and you can display various metrics, such as the coefficients, p-values, and R-squared value.

2. **Signal Processing Toolbox**: This toolbox provides tools for analyzing, filtering, and transforming signals. It includes functions for spectral analysis, filtering, and signal

generation. It is widely used in applications involving audio, vibration analysis, and communication systems.

Example: **Low-Pass Filter with `lowpass`** The `lowpass` function is used to apply a low-pass filter to a signal, removing frequencies higher than a specified cutoff frequency.

```
fs = 1000;   % Sampling frequency (Hz)
f = 50;      % Frequency of the signal (Hz)
t = 0:1/fs:1; % Time vector (1 second of data)
signal = sin(2*pi*f*t);  % Sine wave signal
filtered_signal = lowpass(signal, 100, fs);  % Apply low-pass filter
with 100 Hz cutoff
```

Here, we create a sine wave signal and apply a low-pass filter with a cutoff frequency of 100 Hz. The `lowpass` function will retain frequencies below 100 Hz and attenuate higher frequencies.

3. **Optimization Toolbox**: The Optimization Toolbox provides functions for solving linear, nonlinear, and mixed-integer optimization problems. It includes functions for constrained and unconstrained optimization, linear programming, and least squares fitting.

Example: **Minimizing a Function with `fminunc`** `fminunc` is used to minimize a function that doesn't have constraints. Here's how you can minimize a simple quadratic function:

```
f = @(x) (x-3).^2;  % Define function to minimize
x_opt = fminunc(f, 0);  % Minimize the function starting from x = 0
disp(x_opt);  % Display the optimized value of x
```

In this example, we minimize the function $f(x)=(x-3)^2$ using `fminunc`. The function starts at $x=0$ and iteratively finds the value of x that minimizes the function.

4. **Image Processing Toolbox**: The Image Processing Toolbox provides functions for image filtering, enhancement, segmentation, and feature extraction. This toolbox is extensively used in fields like computer vision, medical imaging, and remote sensing.

Example: **Edge Detection Using `edge`** MATLAB's `edge` function detects edges in an image using various methods such as Sobel, Prewitt, and Canny edge detection.

```
img = imread('image.jpg');  % Read an image
edges = edge(rgb2gray(img), 'Canny');  % Perform Canny edge detection
imshow(edges);  % Display the edges
```

Here, we read an image, convert it to grayscale, and apply Canny edge detection to find the boundaries of objects within the image.

2. MATLAB vs C: Library Integration and Use

While MATLAB is a high-level programming language designed for ease of use in numerical computing, C is a lower-level language that provides fine-grained control over memory management and performance. C is commonly used in performance-critical applications, whereas MATLAB excels in rapid development, data analysis, and visualization. Both languages can be integrated with each other, allowing users to combine the strengths of both environments.

MATLAB Libraries:

MATLAB provides a large array of built-in functions and specialized toolboxes, making it an excellent choice for high-level data analysis and modeling. These toolboxes come prepackaged, optimized for specific domains, and easy to use. For example:

- **MATLAB Statistics and Machine Learning Toolbox** for statistical analysis and machine learning.
- **MATLAB Signal Processing Toolbox** for filtering, Fourier analysis, and more.
- **MATLAB Optimization Toolbox** for solving linear and nonlinear optimization problems.

Because MATLAB is optimized for rapid prototyping and visualization, it's often preferred when developing and testing algorithms.

C Libraries:

C, on the other hand, is often used for more performance-intensive tasks because it allows for better memory management and computational efficiency. Libraries like **BLAS** (Basic Linear Algebra Subprograms) and **LAPACK** (Linear Algebra PACKage) provide high-performance linear algebra operations.

Though MATLAB is very efficient, there may be cases where you want to leverage the speed of C libraries for tasks such as matrix multiplication, large-scale simulations, or performance-critical algorithms.

Integrating C with MATLAB:

MATLAB allows for the integration of C code through MEX files (MATLAB Executable files). These files are compiled C code that can be directly called from within MATLAB, allowing you to run performance-intensive algorithms written in C while still benefiting from MATLAB's easy-to-use syntax and visualization tools.

Example: Calling C code from MATLAB via MEX

1. First, write the C code (e.g., `myCcode.c`).
2. Compile the C code into a MEX file using the `mex` command in MATLAB:

```
mex myCcode.c  % Compile the C code into a MEX file
```

3. Once compiled, you can call the C code from MATLAB like any other function:

```
result = myCcode(input_data);  % Call the compiled C code
```

The `mex` command creates a MEX file, which MATLAB can call as if it were a native function. This allows MATLAB users to write critical performance parts of their program in C, while still working within MATLAB's high-level environment for other tasks.

9.3 Optimization and Performance Tuning

MATLAB is an excellent tool for numerical and scientific computing. However, when working with large datasets or computationally intensive tasks, performance can become a bottleneck. To address these challenges, MATLAB offers various techniques and strategies for optimizing code execution. Key strategies include **vectorization**, **algorithm optimization**, and **parallel computing**. Let's dive into each of these methods in detail.

1. Speeding Up Code with Vectorization

Vectorization refers to the process of converting iterative loops (such as `for` loops) into matrix or vector operations. MATLAB is optimized to handle matrix and vector operations much faster than loops. This is because MATLAB uses highly optimized libraries like BLAS (Basic Linear Algebra Subprograms) to perform these operations, which makes the code run much faster.

Using vectorized operations, MATLAB is able to process entire arrays or matrices in a single step, leveraging internal optimizations to improve performance.

Example: Without and With Vectorization

Without Vectorization (using a loop):

```
n = 1000;
A = zeros(1, n);
for i = 1:n
    A(i) = i^2;  % Squaring each element in the loop
end
```

In this example, a loop is used to compute the square of each element from `1` to `1000`. This is slow because the loop iterates over every element and performs the calculation one-by-one.

With Vectorization (using matrix operations):

```
n = 1000;
A = (1:n).^2;  % Vectorized approach, calculates squares in one step
```

By vectorizing the operation, we can calculate the squares of all numbers in one command. MATLAB's internal handling of this operation is highly efficient and runs much faster than using loops.

Why vectorization works:

- MATLAB's internal implementation for matrix operations is highly optimized.
- Vectorized operations minimize the overhead caused by interpreting and executing the loop control statements (`for` and `end`).

In general, you should always aim to replace loops with vectorized operations in MATLAB whenever possible.

---

2. Optimizing Algorithms in MATLAB

Optimizing your code involves not just vectorizing loops, but also improving the overall design of your algorithms. Here are some techniques to optimize algorithms in MATLAB:

A. Avoiding Repeated Calculations

If the same calculation is being done multiple times in your code, you can store the result in a variable to avoid redundant computations. This can help reduce execution time, especially in large-scale applications.

Example:

```
% Inefficient code with repeated calculation
result1 = some_function(x);
result2 = some_function(x);   % Same calculation repeated

% Optimized code: store the result
result = some_function(x);
result1 = result;
result2 = result;   % Avoid duplicate computation
```

By storing the result of a computation that's used multiple times, you eliminate the need to recalculate the same value, thus improving efficiency.

B. Pre-allocating Arrays

In MATLAB, dynamically resizing arrays inside loops (e.g., appending elements to an array in each iteration) can significantly slow down performance. Pre-allocating the array with a fixed size before entering the loop ensures that MATLAB allocates memory for the array in one go, avoiding the overhead associated with resizing.

Example:

```
n = 1000;
A = zeros(1, n);   % Pre-allocate an array of size n
for i = 1:n
    A(i) = i^2;   % Fill the array without resizing
end
```

In this example, `zeros(1, n)` pre-allocates the array `A` of size `n`, which avoids the overhead of dynamically resizing the array during the loop.

C. Using Built-in Functions

MATLAB's built-in functions are highly optimized, often written in low-level languages like C or Fortran, and make full use of the underlying hardware. Whenever possible, use these built-in functions instead of implementing custom algorithms, as they are more efficient.

Example:

Instead of writing your own sorting algorithm, use the `sort` function, which is highly optimized:

```
A = [3, 1, 4, 1, 5, 9];
sortedA = sort(A);   % MATLAB's optimized sorting function
```

By leveraging built-in functions like `sort`, `mean`, `sum`, `std`, etc., MATLAB can execute these tasks much faster than custom-written code.

---

3. Parallel Computing

Parallel computing is an important technique for accelerating computationally intensive tasks by using multiple CPU cores simultaneously. MATLAB offers tools such as `parfor` (parallel for loops) and `spmd` (Single Program Multiple Data) to enable parallel execution of tasks, significantly speeding up the execution time.

A. Using `parfor` for Parallel Loops

A regular `for` loop runs sequentially, but a `parfor` loop splits the work among multiple cores, allowing computations to be done concurrently. This can lead to substantial performance improvements, particularly for large datasets or tasks that are easily parallelizable.

Example: Using `parfor` to perform parallel computation

```
n = 1000;       .
A = zeros(1, n);
parfor i = 1:n
    A(i) = some_large_computation(i);   % Each iteration runs in parallel
end
```

In this example, the computation is distributed across multiple CPU cores, with each core processing different iterations of the loop simultaneously.

Key Points about `parfor`:

- The iterations of the loop are independent (i.e., there's no dependency between iterations).
- `parfor` divides the work among available CPU cores and runs each iteration in parallel.
- Not all loops can be parallelized — `parfor` only works when iterations are independent.

B. Using `spmd` for Parallel Execution

The `spmd` (Single Program Multiple Data) construct in MATLAB allows you to run the same program on multiple workers with different data. This is useful for more complex parallel tasks where workers need to execute the same code but with different data sets.

```
parpool(4);   % Start a pool of 4 workers
spmd
    % Each worker gets its own portion of the data
    disp(['I am worker ', num2str(gcf)]);
end
```

This method provides fine-grained control over parallel computation, especially when you need to manage shared resources or data between workers.

25 multiple-choice questions (MCQs)

9.1 MATLAB Functions for Data Analysis

Matrix Manipulations, Eigenvalues, and Linear Algebra

1. **What function is used to calculate the eigenvalues of a matrix in MATLAB?**
   - a) eig()
   - b) eigen()
   - c) inv()
   - d) svd()
   - **Answer:** a) eig()
2. **Which of the following commands will transpose a matrix A in MATLAB?**
   - a) A.'
   - b) transpose(A)
   - c) A.transpose()
   - d) Both a and b
   - **Answer:** d) Both a and b
3. **Which operator is used to solve linear systems in MATLAB?**
   - a) *
   - b) /
   - c) ^
   - d) \

o **Answer:** d) \

4. **Which function is used to create a matrix where the sum of each row and column equals the same constant?**
    o a) ones()
    o b) magic()
    o c) rand()
    o d) eye()
    o **Answer:** b) magic()

5. **In MATLAB, how do you add two matrices, A and B, element-wise?**
    o a) A + B
    o b) add(A, B)
    o c) A + B()
    o d) matrixadd(A, B)
    o **Answer:** a) A + B

6. **What does the MATLAB function 'svd()' compute?**
    o a) Singular Value Decomposition
    o b) Eigenvalue Decomposition
    o c) LU Decomposition
    o d) QR Decomposition
    o **Answer:** a) Singular Value Decomposition

Built-in MATLAB Functions for Numerical Methods

7. **Which function in MATLAB is used to perform numerical integration using Simpson's rule?**
    o a) trapz()
    o b) integrate()
    o c) quad()
    o d) integral()
    o **Answer:** d) integral()

8. **What function would you use in MATLAB to approximate the derivative of a function?**
    o a) diff()
    o b) derivate()
    o c) gradient()
    o d) derivative()
    o **Answer:** a) diff()

9. **Which MATLAB function is used to interpolate data points in one dimension?**
    o a) interp2()
    o b) interp1()
    o c) spline()
    o d) polyfit()
    o **Answer:** b) interp1()

10. **Which MATLAB function can be used for numerical optimization of an unconstrained function?**
    o a) fminbnd()
    o b) fminunc()

- o c) fmincon()
- o d) fminsearch()
- o **Answer:** b) fminunc()

9.2 Using External Libraries and Toolboxes

Exploring MATLAB Toolboxes

11. **Which toolbox in MATLAB provides functions for statistical analysis and machine learning?**
    - o a) Signal Processing Toolbox
    - o b) Statistics and Machine Learning Toolbox
    - o c) Image Processing Toolbox
    - o d) Optimization Toolbox
    - o **Answer:** b) Statistics and Machine Learning Toolbox

12. **What function in the Signal Processing Toolbox is used to apply a low-pass filter to a signal?**
    - o a) filter()
    - o b) lowpass()
    - o c) fft()
    - o d) bandpass()
    - o **Answer:** b) lowpass()

13. **Which of the following is NOT part of the MATLAB Image Processing Toolbox?**
    - o a) imresize()
    - o b) imshow()
    - o c) imrotate()
    - o d) filter2()
    - o **Answer:** d) filter2()

14. **The Optimization Toolbox in MATLAB is used for which of the following?**
    - o a) Signal filtering
    - o b) Statistical analysis
    - o c) Solving optimization problems
    - o d) Numerical integration
    - o **Answer:** c) Solving optimization problems

15. **Which function in MATLAB's Statistics and Machine Learning Toolbox is used to fit a linear regression model?**
    - o a) lmfit()
    - o b) regfit()
    - o c) fitlm()
    - o d) regress()
    - o **Answer:** c) fitlm()

16. **In the MATLAB Signal Processing Toolbox, which function is used to compute the Fast Fourier Transform (FFT) of a signal?**
    - o a) fft()
    - o b) ifft()

- ○ c) fft2()
- ○ d) fftshift()
- ○ **Answer:** a) fft()

17. **What is the primary use of the MATLAB Image Processing Toolbox?**
    - ○ a) 3D visualization
    - ○ b) Image transformation and filtering
    - ○ c) Numerical integration
    - ○ d) Linear regression
    - ○ **Answer:** b) Image transformation and filtering

18. **Which of the following MATLAB toolboxes is specifically designed for financial applications?**
    - ○ a) Image Processing Toolbox
    - ○ b) Financial Toolbox
    - ○ c) Optimization Toolbox
    - ○ d) Signal Processing Toolbox
    - ○ **Answer:** b) Financial Toolbox

MATLAB vs C: Library Integration and Use

19. **What is a major advantage of using MATLAB over C for data analysis tasks?**
    - ○ a) MATLAB is faster for low-level memory manipulation
    - ○ b) MATLAB is better suited for scientific computing and data visualization
    - ○ c) MATLAB is used for performance-critical tasks
    - ○ d) C is not useful for numerical computing
    - ○ **Answer:** b) MATLAB is better suited for scientific computing and data visualization

20. **To call C functions in MATLAB, which tool is used to compile C code into a form MATLAB can execute?**
    - ○ a) MEX (MATLAB Executable) functions
    - ○ b) Coder
    - ○ c) mexcompile
    - ○ d) MATLAB Compiler
    - ○ **Answer:** a) MEX (MATLAB Executable) functions

9.3 Optimization and Performance Tuning

Speeding Up Code with Vectorization

21. **What is the primary benefit of vectorization in MATLAB?**
    - ○ a) Makes the code easier to read
    - ○ b) Reduces memory usage
    - ○ c) Increases the speed of execution
    - ○ d) Improves code portability
    - ○ **Answer:** c) Increases the speed of execution

22. **Which MATLAB command is an example of a vectorized operation?**
    - ○ a) A(i) = i^2;

- o b) A = (1:n).^2;
- o c) for i = 1:n, A(i) = i^2; end
- o d) None of the above
- o **Answer:** b) A = (1:n).^2;

23. **Which of the following is NOT an advantage of vectorized operations in MATLAB?**
    - o a) Faster execution
    - o b) Increased clarity of the code
    - o c) Enhanced memory usage
    - o d) Faster development times
    - o **Answer:** c) Enhanced memory usage

24. **In the context of optimization, which method is preferred for matrix operations in MATLAB?**
    - o a) Using for loops
    - o b) Vectorization
    - o c) Manual memory management
    - o d) Using external libraries like BLAS
    - o **Answer:** b) Vectorization

Optimizing Algorithms in MATLAB

25. **What is a common technique for improving the performance of algorithms in MATLAB?**
    - o a) Using dynamic arrays
    - o b) Pre-allocating memory for arrays
    - o c) Using recursive functions
    - o d) Writing all code in C
    - o **Answer:** b) Pre-allocating memory for arrays

9.1 MATLAB Functions for Data Analysis

Matrix Manipulations, Eigenvalues, and Linear Algebra

1. **Question:** Write a MATLAB code to calculate the eigenvalues and eigenvectors of a given 3x3 matrix A = [4 -2 1; 1 6 -1; 2 1 5].

   Answer:

```
A = [4 -2 1; 1 6 -1; 2 1 5];
[eigenvectors, eigenvalues] = eig(A);
disp('Eigenvalues:');
disp(diag(eigenvalues));
disp('Eigenvectors:');
disp(eigenvectors);
```

2. **Question:** Write a MATLAB code to perform matrix multiplication between two matrices A = [1 2; 3 4] and B = [5 6; 7 8].

Answer:

```
A = [1 2; 3 4];
B = [5 6; 7 8];
C = A * B;
disp('Matrix multiplication result:');
disp(C);
```

3. **Question:** Write a MATLAB code to transpose the matrix `A = [1 2 3; 4 5 6]` and store the result in matrix `B`.

    Answer:

    ```
    A = [1 2 3; 4 5 6];
    B = A.';   % Transpose of A
    disp('Transposed matrix:');
    disp(B);
    ```

4. **Question:** Write a MATLAB function to solve the linear system `Ax = b` where `A = [3 2; 1 4]` and `b = [5; 6]`.

    Answer:

    ```
    function x = solveLinearSystem(A, b)
        x = A\b;
    end
    % Calling the function
    A = [3 2; 1 4];
    b = [5; 6];
    solution = solveLinearSystem(A, b);
    disp('Solution to the system:');
    disp(solution);
    ```

5. **Question:** Write a MATLAB code to create a 5x5 identity matrix.

    Answer:

    ```
    identity_matrix = eye(5);
    disp('5x5 Identity matrix:');
    disp(identity_matrix);
    ```

Built-in MATLAB Functions for Numerical Methods

6. **Question:** Write a MATLAB code to perform numerical integration of `f(x) = x^2` between `0` and `1`.

    Answer:

    ```
    f = @(x) x.^2;
    integral_value = integral(f, 0, 1);
    ```

```
disp('Numerical integration result:');
disp(integral_value);
```

7. **Question:** Write a MATLAB code to approximate the derivative of the function `f(x) =` `x^2` at `x = 2` using the `diff()` function.

Answer:

```
f = @(x) x.^2;
x = linspace(1, 3, 100);   % Generate x values
y = f(x);   % Calculate function values
dy = diff(y) ./ diff(x);   % Numerical derivative
approx_derivative_at_2 = dy(find(x == 2));
disp('Approximate derivative at x = 2:');
disp(approx_derivative_at_2);
```

8. **Question:** Write a MATLAB code to perform 1D interpolation on the data points `x = [1 2 3 4]` and `y = [2 4 6 8]` at `x = 2.5`.

Answer:

```
x = [1 2 3 4];
y = [2 4 6 8];
y_interp = interp1(x, y, 2.5);   % Interpolate at x = 2.5
disp('Interpolated value at x = 2.5:');
disp(y_interp);
```

9.2 Using External Libraries and Toolboxes

Exploring MATLAB Toolboxes

9. **Question:** Write a MATLAB code using the Statistics and Machine Learning Toolbox to fit a linear regression model to the data `X = [1 2 3 4 5]` and `Y = [2 4 6 8 10]`.

Answer:

```
X = [1 2 3 4 5]';
Y = [2 4 6 8 10]';
mdl = fitlm(X, Y);   % Fit a linear regression model
disp('Linear regression model:');
disp(mdl);
```

10. **Question:** Write a MATLAB code using the Signal Processing Toolbox to filter a signal using a low-pass filter with a cutoff frequency of 100 Hz.

Answer:

```
fs = 1000;   % Sampling frequency
f = 50;      % Frequency of the signal
```

```
t = 0:1/fs:1;   % Time vector
signal = sin(2*pi*f*t);   % Sine wave signal
filtered_signal = lowpass(signal, 100, fs);   % Apply low-pass filter
plot(t, filtered_signal);
title('Filtered Signal');
xlabel('Time (s)');
ylabel('Amplitude');
```

11. **Question:** Write a MATLAB code using the Optimization Toolbox to minimize the function `f(x) = (x-3)^2` starting at `x = 0`.

Answer:

```
f = @(x) (x-3).^2;   % Define the function
x_opt = fminunc(f, 0);   % Minimize the function
disp('Optimal value of x:');
disp(x_opt);
```

12. **Question:** Write a MATLAB code to read an image file (`image.jpg`) and convert it to grayscale using the Image Processing Toolbox.

Answer:

```
img = imread('image.jpg');   % Read image file
gray_img = rgb2gray(img);   % Convert to grayscale
imshow(gray_img);   % Display the grayscale image
title('Grayscale Image');
```

9.3 Optimization and Performance Tuning

Speeding Up Code with Vectorization

13. **Question:** Write a MATLAB code to calculate the squares of the first 1000 numbers using a loop and then using vectorization. Compare the performance.

Answer:

```
% Using loop
n = 1000;
A = zeros(1, n);
for i = 1:n
    A(i) = i^2;
end

% Using vectorization
B = (1:n).^2;

disp('Squares of first 1000 numbers (using loop):');
disp(A(1:10));
disp('Squares of first 1000 numbers (using vectorization):');
```

```
disp(B(1:10));
```

14. **Question:** Write a MATLAB code to compute the sum of elements of a large matrix `A = rand(1000, 1000)` without using loops.

Answer:

```
A = rand(1000, 1000);
sum_A = sum(A(:));   % Vectorized sum of all elements
disp('Sum of all elements in A:');
disp(sum_A);
```

Optimizing Algorithms in MATLAB

15. **Question:** Write a MATLAB code to demonstrate the performance improvement of pre-allocating an array versus dynamically resizing it within a loop.

Answer:

```
% Without pre-allocation
n = 10000;
A = [];
tic;
for i = 1:n
    A(i) = i^2;
end
toc;

% With pre-allocation
B = zeros(1, n);
tic;
for i = 1:n
    B(i) = i^2;
end
toc;
```

CHAPTER 10: EXERCISES AND CASE STUDIES

10.1 Practice Problems: Translating C Code to MATLAB

Translating code from C to MATLAB is a fundamental exercise that helps you bridge the gap between two programming languages used extensively for scientific and engineering computations. While both C and MATLAB can handle matrix-based operations, there are some key differences in syntax, data structures, and functions that you need to be aware of when making the translation.

Step-by-Step Solutions and Insights

When translating **C code** to **MATLAB**, there are four main steps you should follow:

1. **Identify C Data Structures and Their Equivalents in MATLAB**
   - **Arrays in C** are typically one-dimensional or multi-dimensional arrays. In MATLAB, **arrays** (also known as **vectors** or **matrices**) can hold numbers in similar ways, and MATLAB handles both row and column vectors efficiently.
     - Example: `int arr[10];` in C would be equivalent to `arr = zeros(1, 10);` or `arr = ones(1, 10);` in MATLAB.
     - Example for multi-dimensional arrays in C (`int arr[3][3];` in C):
       - MATLAB: `arr = zeros(3, 3);`
   - **For Loops in C**: MATLAB supports **for loops** similar to C, but MATLAB has built-in matrix operations and functions that can replace many iterative tasks, making the code faster and more efficient.
   - **Memory Management**: MATLAB handles memory dynamically, so you don't need to manually allocate or free memory like in C.
2. **Handle Functions**
   - **MATLAB Functions**: MATLAB allows you to define functions with flexible inputs and outputs. Functions can be defined inline or separately, and MATLAB also supports **anonymous functions**.
   - **Rewriting Array Functions**: MATLAB provides built-in functions for common operations like `sum`, `prod`, `mean`, `std`, etc. These functions work directly with matrices and vectors without the need for manual iteration (loops).
3. **Translate Control Structures**
   - **If-Else Statements**: MATLAB's `if-else` syntax is quite similar to C, but more compact:
     - Example in C:

```
if (x > 0) {
    printf("Positive\n");
} else {
    printf("Negative\n");
}
```

     - MATLAB equivalent:

```
if x > 0
    disp('Positive');
```

```
    else
        disp('Negative');
    end
```

- o **For Loops**: MATLAB loops work similarly to C, but more often you can replace loops with matrix-based operations (vectorization), which improves performance.
- o **While Loops**: These are used the same way in both C and MATLAB, although MATLAB offers some alternatives like `for` loops, `arrayfun`, and `cellfun`.

4. **Consider MATLAB's Vectorization**
   - o **Vectorization** is one of MATLAB's core strengths. Instead of iterating over arrays with loops, you can often apply a function to an entire matrix or vector, significantly improving performance.
   - o Example: Replacing a **for loop** in C with **vectorized code** in MATLAB:

Example: Translating C Code to MATLAB

Let's consider a **simple example** of translating C code that computes the sum of the squares of the first 100 integers.

C Code Example:

```c
#include <stdio.h>

int main() {
    int sum = 0;
    for (int i = 1; i <= 100; i++) {
        sum += i * i;
    }
    printf("The sum of squares is: %d\n", sum);
    return 0;
}
```

This C program loops through integers from 1 to 100 and computes the sum of their squares. The result is printed using `printf`.

MATLAB Code Equivalent:

In MATLAB, we can use a loop in a similar way to compute the sum of squares:

```matlab
sum = 0;
for i = 1:100
    sum = sum + i^2;
end
disp(['The sum of squares is: ', num2str(sum)]);
```

This MATLAB code does the same thing as the C code, but the syntax is a little different. The key differences:

- In MATLAB, `disp` is used to display output.

- MATLAB uses `num2str` to convert numbers to strings when concatenating them with other strings.

Optimized MATLAB Version (Vectorized Code):

MATLAB allows you to **vectorize** the operation, which eliminates the need for explicit loops. This is not only cleaner but can also lead to faster execution.

```
sum_squares = sum((1:100).^2);
disp(['The sum of squares is: ', num2str(sum_squares)]);
```

In this optimized version:

- We create a vector `1:100` representing the integers from `1` to `100`.
- The **element-wise power operation** `.^2` computes the square of each element in the vector.
- The `sum` function adds up all the squared elements.
- This version does not need an explicit loop, and MATLAB can execute it much more efficiently, especially for large datasets.

Key Insights for Translating C to MATLAB:

1. **Simpler Syntax**: MATLAB code is often more concise and easier to read than C, especially for matrix and array operations.
2. **Vectorization**: MATLAB is optimized for matrix and vector operations. You can often replace **for loops** with vectorized operations for performance gains.
3. **Built-in Functions**: MATLAB has a large library of built-in functions for common operations such as `sum`, `mean`, `prod`, `std`, `sort`, etc., making it easier to perform complex operations without coding them manually.
4. **Memory Management**: Unlike C, you don't need to worry about manual memory allocation in MATLAB. It handles dynamic memory allocation internally.
5. **Faster Prototyping**: MATLAB's high-level nature and built-in functions make it excellent for quickly prototyping algorithms or solving mathematical problems, especially in scientific computing and engineering.

10.2 Real-World Applications

MATLAB is an incredibly powerful tool used across a wide range of industries and applications, particularly in engineering, data analysis, and signal processing. It allows professionals to simulate systems, visualize complex data, and process signals with ease, making it an essential tool in various fields such as aerospace, control systems, mechanical engineering, electrical circuits, civil engineering, and more.

Solving Engineering Problems Using MATLAB

MATLAB's built-in functions and toolboxes provide solutions to many complex engineering problems, from simulating dynamic systems to analyzing electrical circuits. Below, we explore how MATLAB can be used to solve engineering problems.

Example 1: Solving a Simple Differential Equation

One of the most common problems in engineering is solving differential equations that model physical systems. MATLAB provides a variety of solvers for these types of equations, with **ode45** being a popular choice for solving first-order ordinary differential equations.

Let's consider a first-order linear differential equation:

$$\frac{dy}{dt} = -2y + 3$$

The solution to this equation can be found using MATLAB's **ode45** function, which is a numerical solver for ordinary differential equations.

MATLAB Code:

```
% Define the differential equation as a function
ode = @(t, y) -2*y + 3;

% Initial condition
y0 = 0;

% Time span for the solution
t_span = [0 5];

% Solve the ODE using ode45
[t, y] = ode45(ode, t_span, y0);

% Plot the solution
plot(t, y);
title('Solution to dy/dt = -2y + 3');
xlabel('Time');
ylabel('y(t)');
```

Explanation:

- **ode**: This defines the differential equation to solve.
- **ode45**: This is MATLAB's solver for ordinary differential equations, which numerically solves the equation over a specified time interval.
- The plot shows the solution $y(t)$ over time, demonstrating how MATLAB can be used to simulate and visualize dynamic systems.

Example 2: Electrical Circuit Analysis (RC Circuit)

MATLAB is widely used in electrical engineering to simulate and analyze electrical circuits. Consider a simple RC (Resistor-Capacitor) circuit where the voltage across the capacitor decays over time as it discharges.

The voltage decay in an RC circuit is governed by the equation:

$$V(t) = V_0 \cdot \exp\left(\frac{-t}{RC}\right)$$

Where:

- V_0 is the initial voltage
- R is the resistance
- C is the capacitance
- t is time

MATLAB Code:

```
R = 1000; % resistance in ohms
C = 1e-6; % capacitance in farads
t = linspace(0, 0.01, 100); % time from 0 to 0.01 seconds
V0 = 5; % initial voltage

% Voltage decay equation
V = V0 * exp(-t/(R*C));

% Plot the voltage across the capacitor
plot(t, V);
title('Voltage Across Capacitor in an RC Circuit');
xlabel('Time (s)');
ylabel('Voltage (V)');
```

Explanation:

- **R** and **C** define the parameters of the circuit.
- **t** is the time vector for the simulation.
- **V** computes the voltage at each time point using the RC discharge equation.
- The plot visualizes the voltage decay across the capacitor.

This example shows how MATLAB can be used to solve electrical circuit problems by simulating the behavior of components such as resistors and capacitors over time.

Simulations, Data Visualization, and Signal Processing

MATLAB excels at simulations, which are widely used in engineering and scientific research. Its powerful toolboxes for **signal processing** allow for detailed analysis and simulation of signals, including noise removal, filtering, and more.

Example 1: Signal Generation and Noise Removal

In real-world applications, signals are often contaminated with noise, and it is important to clean up these signals for further analysis. MATLAB provides excellent tools for signal generation, noise simulation, and filtering.

In this example, we generate a **sine wave** signal, add **Gaussian noise**, and then apply a **low-pass filter** to remove the noise.

MATLAB Code:

```
fs = 1000; % Sampling frequency
t = 0:1/fs:1-1/fs; % Time vector (1 second duration)
f = 50; % Signal frequency

% Generate a sine wave
signal = sin(2*pi*f*t);

% Add Gaussian noise to the signal
noisy_signal = signal + 0.5 * randn(size(t));

% Apply a low-pass filter to remove the noise
filtered_signal = lowpass(noisy_signal, 100, fs);

% Plot the original, noisy, and filtered signals
subplot(3,1,1);
plot(t, signal);
title('Original Signal');

subplot(3,1,2);
plot(t, noisy_signal);
title('Noisy Signal');

subplot(3,1,3);
plot(t, filtered_signal);
title('Filtered Signal');
```

Explanation:

- **fs**: Defines the sampling frequency, meaning how often data points are taken per second.
- **signal**: A sine wave with a frequency of 50 Hz.
- **noisy_signal**: The sine wave signal is corrupted by Gaussian noise (generated using `randn`).
- **lowpass**: A built-in MATLAB function that applies a low-pass filter to remove high-frequency noise.
- The **subplot** command is used to display the original, noisy, and filtered signals in separate panels.

This example demonstrates how MATLAB can be used to generate, manipulate, and clean up signals, making it an essential tool in communications, audio processing, and other signal-related fields.

10.3 Advanced Exercises for Further Learning

MATLAB and C are both powerful tools in computational and scientific programming, but each has its strengths. MATLAB is excellent for rapid prototyping, data visualization, and matrix manipulation, while C is known for its efficiency and performance when handling computationally intensive tasks. By combining these two languages, you can leverage the strengths of both to optimize performance and maintain flexibility.

Using C and MATLAB Together: MEX Files

To combine the computational power of C with the high-level ease of use of MATLAB, MATLAB offers a feature called **MEX** (MATLAB Executable) files. MEX files allow you to write C functions and call them directly from MATLAB. This is particularly useful for tasks that require significant computation, such as numerical simulations, large matrix operations, or tasks that need to be executed repeatedly in a loop. By writing the heavy computational parts of your code in C and calling them from MATLAB, you can achieve the best of both worlds: fast performance and MATLAB's rich set of built-in functions.

1. Example: Using a C Function in MATLAB

Suppose you have a simple task of adding two numbers, and you want to perform the addition in C for performance reasons. You can write a C function that adds two numbers and then call it directly from MATLAB using a MEX file.

C Code (add_numbers.c):

```
#include "mex.h"

// MEX function to add two numbers
void mexFunction(int nlhs, mxArray *plhs[], int nrhs, const mxArray *prhs[])
{
    // Retrieve the input arguments
    double num1 = mxGetScalar(prhs[0]);
    double num2 = mxGetScalar(prhs[1]);

    // Create the output argument (sum of the two numbers)
    plhs[0] = mxCreateDoubleScalar(num1 + num2);
}
```

Explanation:

- The `mexFunction` is the entry point for MEX files. It is always defined this way when writing a MEX function.
- `prhs[]` contains the input arguments passed from MATLAB, and `plhs[]` contains the output arguments returned to MATLAB.
- `mxGetScalar` is used to retrieve scalar values from the MATLAB input arguments.
- `mxCreateDoubleScalar` is used to create the output that will be returned to MATLAB.

Compiling the C code into a MEX file:

In MATLAB, you can compile the C code into a MEX file using the `mex` command:

```
mex add_numbers.c
```

This will create a MEX file (e.g., `add_numbers.mex`), which is a binary file that can be executed by MATLAB.

Calling the MEX function from MATLAB:

Now that the C function is compiled into a MEX file, you can call it from MATLAB as if it were a regular MATLAB function.

```
result = add_numbers(3, 5);
disp(['The sum is: ', num2str(result)]);
```

Output:

```
The sum is: 8
```

This example demonstrates how to write a simple C function, compile it into a MEX file, and use it from MATLAB. It's a simple operation, but the same principle can be applied to more complex algorithms.

2. Example 2: Large-Scale Simulations with C and MATLAB

In some advanced applications, computationally intensive simulations (such as Monte Carlo simulations, numerical solvers, or large-scale matrix computations) are best written in C for performance reasons. MATLAB can then be used for data analysis, visualization, and further processing of the results.

For example, consider a Monte Carlo simulation for estimating the value of π. While MATLAB is capable of performing such simulations, implementing it in C can make the process faster, especially for large-scale simulations.

Step 1: Write the Monte Carlo Simulation in C

In this example, we will create a Monte Carlo simulation that estimates the value of π by randomly generating points inside a square and counting how many fall within a circle. The fraction of points inside the circle gives an estimate for π.

C Code (monte_carlo_pi.c):

```
#include "mex.h"
#include <stdlib.h>
#include <math.h>
```

```c
// MEX function for Monte Carlo simulation to estimate pi
void mexFunction(int nlhs, mxArray *plhs[], int nrhs, const mxArray *prhs[])
{
    // Get the number of points to simulate
    int num_points = mxGetScalar(prhs[0]);

    // Seed random number generator
    srand(0);

    int inside_circle = 0;

    // Simulate points
    for (int i = 0; i < num_points; i++) {
        double x = (double)rand() / RAND_MAX;
        double y = (double)rand() / RAND_MAX;
        if (x*x + y*y <= 1) {
            inside_circle++;
        }
    }

    // Estimate pi
    double pi_estimate = 4.0 * inside_circle / num_points;

    // Return the estimate of pi
    plhs[0] = mxCreateDoubleScalar(pi_estimate);
}
```

Explanation:

- **rand()** generates random numbers between 0 and 1.
- **$xx + yy <= 1$** checks whether the point (x, y) lies inside the unit circle.
- **4.0 * inside_circle / num_points** calculates the estimated value of π.
- The function takes the number of points as an input and returns the estimate of π.

Step 2: Compile the C code into a MEX file

```
mex monte_carlo_pi.c
```

Step 3: Use the MEX function in MATLAB

Now, you can use this C function in MATLAB to run the Monte Carlo simulation.

```
num_points = 1000000;   % Number of random points
pi_estimate = monte_carlo_pi(num_points);
disp(['Estimated value of pi: ', num2str(pi_estimate)]);
```

Output (depends on the random points generated):

```
Estimated value of pi: 3.1416
```

Explanation:

- We call the `monte_carlo_pi` MEX function in MATLAB, passing the number of points to simulate.
- The result is the estimated value of π, which should converge to the true value as the number of points increases.

Why Combine C and MATLAB?

The key advantage of combining C and MATLAB is **performance optimization**. MATLAB is highly efficient for data analysis, visualization, and prototyping, but C can handle computationally heavy tasks more efficiently. By combining the two, you can:

1. **Leverage C's performance**: For tasks that require significant computation, such as numerical simulations, matrix operations, or data processing, C is faster.
2. **Benefit from MATLAB's ease of use**: Once the computationally expensive parts are handled by C, MATLAB can be used for high-level analysis, plotting, and results interpretation.
3. **Integrate existing C code into MATLAB**: If you already have C code, you can bring it into MATLAB without rewriting everything, thus saving time and effort.

APPENDICES

A.1 MATLAB Syntax Reference

MATLAB is a high-level language designed primarily for numerical computing, matrix operations, and data analysis. Its syntax is designed to be user-friendly, especially for engineers and scientists who need to perform complex calculations without having to deal with low-level programming intricacies. Below are some key MATLAB commands and functions that are essential for anyone learning or using MATLAB.

Key MATLAB Commands and Functions:

1. **Variable Assignment:**
   - MATLAB uses the equals sign (=) for variable assignment, which is similar to many other programming languages.

   ```
   x = 5;    % Assign 5 to variable x
   ```

2. **Arithmetic Operations:**
   - MATLAB supports basic arithmetic operations such as addition, subtraction, multiplication, division, and exponentiation.

   ```
   sum = 3 + 4;        % Addition
   difference = 5 - 2; % Subtraction
   product = 3 * 4;    % Multiplication
   quotient = 10 / 2;  % Division
   power = 2^3;        % Exponentiation
   ```

3. **Matrix and Array Operations:**
   - MATLAB is particularly strong in matrix manipulation, and you can create matrices using square brackets ([]).

   ```
   A = [1 2; 3 4];  % Create a 2x2 matrix
   B = [5 6; 7 8];  % Create another 2x2 matrix
   C = A * B;       % Matrix multiplication
   D = A + B;       % Matrix addition
   ```

4. **Control Structures:**
   - MATLAB uses common control structures like if, else, for, and while for conditional and iterative programming.

   ```
   % Conditional statement
   if x > 10
       disp('x is greater than 10');
   else
       disp('x is not greater than 10');
   end

   % For loop
   for i = 1:5
   ```

```
        disp(i);
end

% While loop
while x < 10
    x = x + 1;
end
```

5. **Functions:**
   - o MATLAB functions can be defined using the `function` keyword.

```
function result = add(a, b)
    result = a + b;
end
```

6. **Built-in Functions:**
   - o MATLAB has a vast set of built-in functions for common tasks.

```
mean_value = mean([1, 2, 3, 4, 5]);    % Calculate the mean
std_value = std([1, 2, 3, 4, 5]);      % Calculate the standard
deviation
plot(x, y);                            % Plot data
```

7. **Plotting:**
   - o MATLAB provides powerful plotting capabilities.

```
x = 0:0.1:10;
y = sin(x);
plot(x, y);                            % Simple 2D plot
title('Sine Function');
xlabel('x');
ylabel('y');
```

A.2 C Programming Syntax Reference

C is a lower-level language compared to MATLAB and is designed to provide more control over hardware and system resources. C programming is often used for performance-critical applications. Here are some key aspects of C syntax that are important when transitioning from MATLAB.

Key Differences Between MATLAB and C Syntax:

1. **Variable Declaration:**
   - o In C, you must declare the type of each variable explicitly, whereas in MATLAB, variables are dynamically typed.

```
int x = 5;  // Integer variable in C
double y = 3.14;  // Floating-point variable in C
```

2. Array and Matrix Representation:

- In C, arrays are contiguous memory blocks, and matrix operations are not natively supported as in MATLAB. You need to use loops or external libraries to manipulate arrays.

```
int A[2][2] = {{1, 2}, {3, 4}};  // Declare a 2x2 matrix in C
```

3. Control Structures:

- Both C and MATLAB support if, else, for, and while, but the syntax differs.

```
// If-else in C
if (x > 10) {
    printf("x is greater than 10\n");
} else {
    printf("x is not greater than 10\n");
}

// For loop in C
for (int i = 0; i < 5; i++) {
    printf("%d\n", i);
}

// While loop in C
while (x < 10) {
    x++;
}
```

4. Functions:

- Functions in C are defined with a return type and an explicit parameter list, unlike MATLAB's more flexible function definitions.

```
int add(int a, int b) {
    return a + b;
}
```

5. Arrays and Matrices:

- Arrays in C are fixed in size, and MATLAB has built-in functions for matrix operations. In C, you have to manually implement matrix multiplication, addition, and other operations.

```
// Array in C
int arr[5] = {1, 2, 3, 4, 5};
```

6. Memory Management:

- In C, you have to manage memory manually using functions like malloc and free, while MATLAB handles memory management automatically.

7. No Built-in Plotting:

- Unlike MATLAB, C does not come with built-in plotting capabilities. To plot data, external libraries like gnuplot or SDL are used in C.

A.3 Index of MATLAB Functions and C Code Comparisons

An index of common MATLAB functions and their equivalents in C can help you transition between the two languages more efficiently. Below is a comparison of some commonly used operations in both MATLAB and C.

MATLAB Function	C Equivalent
`mean()`	Manual loop or library function (e.g., `math.h` for average)
`std()`	Manual calculation or use of external libraries
`sum()`	Manual loop to sum array elements
`min()` / `max()`	Loop through array to find min/max
`inv()`	Use an external library like LAPACK or manually implement matrix inversion
`size()`	Use `sizeof` to get array dimensions or manually track size
`reshape()`	Manual array manipulation
`linspace()`	Manual implementation using a loop
`fft()`	Use an external library like FFTW for fast Fourier transforms
`disp()`	`printf()` in C

Example Comparisons:

1. **Finding the Mean of an Array:**
   o **MATLAB:**

```
arr = [1, 2, 3, 4, 5];
mean_val = mean(arr);
```

   o **C:**

```
int arr[] = {1, 2, 3, 4, 5};
int sum = 0;
int n = 5;
for (int i = 0; i < n; i++) {
    sum += arr[i];
}
double mean_val = sum / (double)n;
```

2. Matrix Multiplication:

- **MATLAB:**

```matlab
A = [1, 2; 3, 4];
B = [5, 6; 7, 8];
C = A * B;  % Matrix multiplication
```

- **C:**

```c
int A[2][2] = {{1, 2}, {3, 4}};
int B[2][2] = {{5, 6}, {7, 8}};
int C[2][2];

for (int i = 0; i < 2; i++) {
    for (int j = 0; j < 2; j++) {
        C[i][j] = 0;
        for (int k = 0; k < 2; k++) {
            C[i][j] += A[i][k] * B[k][j];
        }
    }
}
```